ANCESTRAL
MAGIC

Also by Frankie Castanea

Spells for Change

ANCESTRAL MAGIC

A MODERN WITCH'S GUIDE TO FOLK TRADITIONS & RECONNECTION

FRANKIE CASTANEA

First published in Great Britain in 2025 by Orion Spring,
an imprint of The Orion Publishing Group Ltd
Carmelite House, 50 Victoria Embankment

London EC4Y 0DZ

An Hachette UK Company

The authorised representative in the EEA is Hachette Ireland,
8 Castlecourt Centre, Dublin 15, D15 XTP3, Ireland (email: info@hbgi.ie)

1 3 5 7 9 10 8 6 4 2

Copyright © Frankie Castanea 2025

Internal illustrrations by Laura Brett

The moral right of Frankie Castanea to be identified as
the author of this work has been asserted in accordance
with the Copyright, Designs and Patents Act of 1988.

All rights reserved. No part of this publication may be reproduced, stored
in a retrieval system, or transmitted in any form or by any means, electronic,
mechanical, photocopying, recording, or otherwise, without the prior permission
of both the copyright owner and the above publisher of this book.

A CIP catalogue record for this book is
available from the British Library.

ISBN (Hardback) 978 1 3987 1881 4
ISBN (Ebook) 978 1 3987 1882 1
ISBN (Audio) 978 1 3987 1883 8

Design and typeset by goldust design
Printed in Great Britain by Clays Ltd, Elcograf, S.p.A

www.orionbooks.co.uk

Every effort has been made to ensure that the information in this book
is accurate. The information in this book is not intended to replace or
conflict with any medical, legal, financial or other professional advice
given to you. You should consult with your GP or other professional
advisor, as appropriate, before trying any of the remedies or techniques
in this book. Neither the publisher nor author accepts any legal
responsibility for any personal injury or other damage or loss
arising from the use of the information in this book.

For my ancestors

CONTENTS

A Note Before We Start	viii
Introduction: How to Use This Book	1
Accountable Reconnection	3

Part 1
HISTORY AND HOMELAND

	33
Homeland	35
History	42
Diaspora	46

Part 2
THE FOLK AND FINDING COMMUNITY

	53
Who Are the Folk?	55
Reconnecting to the People and Culture	61
Seeking Community and Mentorship	67

Part 3
ANCESTORS, ANCESTRAL PRACTICES, AND PLANT ALLIES

	79
Human Ancestors	81
Non-human Ancestors	83
Spirit Ancestors	85
Piecing Together What You Already Have	87
What is Ancestor Veneration?	93

Saints, Regional and Ancestral Spirits, and Deities	119
Healing Generational Trauma and Lineage	183

Part 4
TRADITION — 195

The Importance of Tradition	197
Tradition as Holidays	202
Tradition as Practice	208
Letting Go of Problematic Traditions	213
Putting Tradition into Practice	217

Part 5
RECONSTRUCTION — 221

We Are Not Our Ancestors	223
Ancestral Belief through a Modern Lens	228
Conclusion: The Diaspora and Reconnection in Action	235
Suggested Reading	238
Bibliography	240
Acknowledgments	244

A NOTE BEFORE WE START

Throughout creating this book, I felt a pressure to make sure that everyone could pull something from it and benefit from it. However, I realized very early on that this was not something that was truly possible. I am one person and only have my personal experience. As you read this book, please remember that *Ancestral Magic* is about my experience with reconnection and the tools I used and am currently using to reclaim and reconnect with my Italian American heritage. I am writing this book in hopes that my experience gives others the tools to help them reconnect as well. I am privileged to have access to numerous resources as my family, culture, and folk practices were not intentionally erased from history. I do not experience racism, sexism, or generational trauma in the way that people of color who may read this book do. Because of this, I am recommending several authors of color and their books or articles in the suggested reading section on page 237, in order to help any readers who feel this book did not fulfill all their needs.

INTRODUCTION:
HOW TO USE THIS BOOK

This book is and was born out of a need to belong. So many of us find fragments of the place our ancestors, our parents, our grandparents and great-grandparents came from within small familial traditions and beliefs. These fragments create many things depending on who you are—a sense of loss, belonging, grief, community, guilt, and so much more. How do we reconcile a past we lost? How do we find our place as we reconnect? How do we cope with past and current atrocities and oppression that culture and people we are connected to face? What do we do with fragments of a culture and a people that we can only grasp at?

We can piece together the fragments. It sounds simple, but like a ceramic plate or dish, the fragments may never look the way they did before they were broken—by colonization, by assimilation, by trauma. Instead of looking to what the plate was before it was broken, I ask you now to imagine what it will look like after it's put together. Will it maintain a similar shape? Will there be pieces missing? Will you use glue or tape to piece it together? Will you paint over it? Will you restore the original color? In what ways will you reconnect with what came before you while also creating something new, something that speaks to you?

In this book we will explore history, homeland, connecting

to the folk, ancestral practices, finding plant allies, and crafting our own traditions. We will deepen and expand our practice beyond its current limits and connect each piece with those who have gone before us.

Many people looking for cultural reconnection are the descendants of diasporas—cultural groups dispersed from their homeland. While some diasporas may have peaceful histories, the ways in which cultures change over time and place is not always pleasant. Many times, culture is taken from people and, oftentimes, this results in descendants being separated from their ancestors' culture. If while reading this you are wondering how you can reconnect with your ancestry without an understanding of who your ancestors are, do not fear. We all come from somewhere—we are born from it, we are adopted into it, and we find it within a community that welcomes us with open arms.

This book is both a recipe and a manual. I add a dash of this and a pinch of that, and you may need to add a dash of that and a pinch of this. It is a guide to push you to look harder, do the work, and begin your journey to reconnecting and restoring your heritage and ancestral practice. Reconnection is not a couple years of research and mentorship—it is a process that takes years of connecting, reading, cross-referencing, and checking yourself. It requires respect, a diligent eye, and self-reflection. Reconnection is a form of rebellion against the wrongs that preceded us and a hopeful mission towards an enriched and inclusive practice. Your journey does not end with this book—it merely begins.

ACCOUNTABLE RECONNECTION

What does accountable reconnection and restoration look like? This question, if you have not yet asked yourself it, should be at the forefront of your mind when starting this book. Accountable reconnection revolves around a few ideas that are kept at the center of your reconnection journey, including: respect for the culture and folk you are reconnecting with, and reconnecting for the right reasons. Respectfully approaching a culture that you are no longer a part of is a central part of this journey—while you may feel pulled to call yourself that which your ancestors did (Irish, Romani, Greek) right off the bat, without taking the steps to familiarize yourself with the folk and culture, there is a risk of appropriation.

"But, Frankie," you may say. "How can I be culturally appropriating from a group of people I am descended from?" I often explain the importance of respect within reconnection through the following metaphor:

A long time ago—let's say eighty to ninety years ago—your great-grandparents lived in a neighborhood. The neighborhood was a community. There were celebrations and holidays specific to the community. Your great-grandparents learned the ins and outs of the neighborhood—the good and the bad. However, after seventy years, your family moved. Perhaps they moved because the neighborhood's resources ran out.

Perhaps they moved away because someone else kicked them out. Perhaps they moved by choice ... or perhaps they didn't. But either way, they moved. At first, your great-grandparents tried to keep in touch with the community they had left. They brought old friends over for tea to share stories about the neighborhood. But as your grandparents grew up, they may have had less interest in learning about the community they left behind. Perhaps they weren't even allowed to learn about the old neighborhood—saying where they were from may have presented a danger to their family, or perhaps they faced violence by trying to learn more about their old ways of being. They carried some ideas, stories, and aspects as they grew up, but they never pursued them further than what they remembered. For some, perhaps engaging with the old neighborhood was done so out of duty, not interest.

Then, when your parent was born, they knew of elements from the neighborhood that your great-grandparents moved away from, but it wasn't the same. Perhaps your parent had no interest in the previous community or its stories, recipes, and holidays and so never sought out anyone to learn more from. Even if they lived in a new neighborhood with others from the old neighborhood, it was different. Something new. By the time you are born, there's a good chance you'll only hear about your great-grandparents' old neighborhood in passing—how different it was, why they moved, and how things have changed, for better or worse. Perhaps your parents or grandparents felt a desire—or necessity—to fit into the new neighborhood. Regardless of their reasons, you are left in a place where you know almost nothing about your great-grandparents' previous community and home. What you do know is stories, ideas, rituals, and other cultural elements from almost a hundred years ago.

This story may be slightly different for everyone who reads it—it may be your grandparents who left the neighborhood, and you may still have friends and family whose doors you can still knock on. You may have been forced out of the neighborhood due to a lack of work in the surrounding areas. Your family may have been kidnapped and stolen from the neighborhood two hundred years ago, and forced into slavery in the new neighborhood. Perhaps the neighborhood everyone else moved into was yours, and you were forcibly removed from your land, as new occupants stole your homes. Maybe your family wasn't even allowed to learn about the old neighborhood, let alone stay in communication with it. Persecution for religious or spiritual beliefs, such as for practicing Judaism or Indigenous spirituality, are another reason why a people may have been driven away from ways of being—for safety and for survival.

This cycle continues and takes place every day in ways we both see and cannot see. For me, the neighborhood is what my family referred to as the "Old Country," or *Sud Italia*," and the new neighborhood we moved to was America. When I was young, I knew little about Italy—I only knew that we had Christmas Eve celebrations with my extended family, my nana always wore a cross, and my grandparents were devout Catholics. I had become a complete stranger to the culture that my great-grandparents belonged to through the process of assimilation into America. I was not raised speaking Italian in my house, I was unfamiliar with Catholicism, and while I was baptized, I never attended church. There was more that my family had lost over the years—folk practices, beliefs, and recipes—that I knew nothing about. Reconnecting with my family's culture required me to strip myself of my ego and avoid feeling as if I was entitled to something that I was no longer a part of. It required me to talk to folks connected with both Italian and Italian American culture to learn more about what we had lost. While my grandma or mother may not have felt a void from the disconnect that I am searching to repair, over time, I began to notice something was missing.

When it comes to reconnection, there is value in connecting to your ancestors' "neighborhood" as much as there is value in understanding the new "neighborhood"—the diaspora. Not every immigrant has the same story, and folk practices and traditions are not always abandoned in the ways that we think they are. While there is obvious necessity in understanding cultures of origin, it is just as important to recognize and validate the cultures that emerge in diasporic communities. An Italian identity will not look the same as an Italian American identity, nor are they required to look the same. Even within different regions of Italy, folk practices and traditions look vastly different from one another. Italy was likely not even a nation-state during some ancestors' immigration, and many immigrated holding the identities of their specific region—Calabrian, Sicilian, Campanian. But this changed over time within diasporic enclaves and collections of immigrants, in part due to members from different regions sharing and transmitting information from their regions to each other. Even then, individuals from different enclaves will have a distinct culture, separate from an Italian American enclave in a different city or country, such as Italian Americans from Chicago versus New York and Italian Americans versus Italian Australians.

While some practices of particular cultures are open, it's still disrespectful to walk into a neighborhood your family hasn't lived in for almost a hundred years and insist you know your way around. Reconnecting to folk practices often requires learning about the culture of origin and recognizing the folk magic that diasporic practices and culture stem from. Even if folk practices carry through a diaspora, learning about the origins of a practice can help you understand the history and context of said practice. The culture and ancestry you are working to reconnect with are not ones you have access to just because of blood ties or because your great-great-grandparent lived in that country, especially if the practices and culture you are working to reconnect to include closed or heavily guarded practices.

Reconnection, as a whole, is a process that focuses on accountability, anti-racism, and respect for the culture and folk you are working to connect with. It's frustrating, anger-inducing, brings about grief, but most of all—it brings about joy. Elation is a product of finding the culture your ancestors lost through trauma, through choice, or through hardship. The process of reconnection allows us to look to our roots rather than seek out closed practices of minorities and feed off of the Western idea of spirituality fueling capitalism and misappropriation of many different religions and cultures.

WHY ARE YOU HERE?

Before we begin our journey with reconnection and ancestors, I want to let you know that this book won't be entirely comfortable. It's not intended to be, because reconnection is not comfortable. I urge you to lean into the discomfort, the grief, and the rage that may accompany this book. I may say things you won't like or I may say things that you've felt ring true for you and your experience for longer than you've been on this journey. Either way, interrogating why you want to reconnect and why you are here is the tip of the iceberg for this book and your personal journey. Allow yourself to breathe deeply and close your eyes if you're comfortable. Ask yourself what you are seeking and why you are embarking on this journey. There isn't a wrong answer. In the space below, write out why you are here.

_____
_____
_____
_____
_____
_____
_____
_____
_____

WHAT TO THINK ABOUT WHEN DOING YOUR OWN RESEARCH

When researching, I like to keep a couple of things in mind, particularly surrounding the topic and the author.

WHO?
Who wrote this paper/book? Are they a reconnecting individual, an ethnographer, a folklorist, someone in the culture, or more than one of these?

How this helps us:
Understanding the way in which an individual, author, or academic is approaching the topic allows us to critically assess the framework that the author/writer is using to write their paper or book. Are they approaching through the lens of someone who has lived within the tradition and/or culture? Are they assessing the way folklore affects the culture? Are they studying the customs of individuals and their culture? Are they approaching this from an outsider's standpoint or an insider's? Will they be respectful of the culture and the individuals in their work, or piece together aspects to serve their own goals, removing them from the cultural context?

WHAT?
What is this paper/book about? In what ways does the author present information? What approach is the paper or book taking?

How this helps us:
To follow on from *who*, we can look at *what*—this helps us critically assess and look at how this book will affect our

beliefs, our practice, and our reconnection journey. We can look at how the author presents information—is more context needed? Is the cultural context given within the work? We can also look at the approach the paper is taking—what is the goal? The question of *what* further expands on the idea of *who* by flushing out the methodology, lens of the author, and context of the work in ways that will help us apply it to our own practice.

WHEN?
When was this paper/book written?

How this helps us:
When the paper/book was written is an imperative part of the research process that is often ignored. Culture and folklore are living and breathing things and they change with the people over time. As new people are born into the culture, the way knowledge and traditions are passed down changes as well. Understanding when the work was written allows us to acknowledge that the topic and context of the work may have changed over time. For example, in the early 1900s in unified Italy, the culture was incredibly Catholic and most of the folk magic was heavily syncretized (amalgamated) with these aspects. Those who immigrated during this time brought the syncretized elements of folk magic with them, and passed them down over time. In modern-day Italy, Dr Angela Puca remarks that there has been an evolution in syncretism and that the newer tradition is more inclined to mesh paganism—rather than the religious aspects of Catholicism—with the folk magic. In this paper, Dr Puca also discusses the newer generation's inclination to identify as witches, rather than the older generation's refusal to be called as such (Puca, 2019).

WHERE?

Where was the information in the paper/book collected from? Where is the individual writing it from? Did they travel to a specific region to create the work?

How this helps us:

Where is one of the most important aspects of learning a text. As reconnectors, we can search and search and search but not find accurate information on cultural or familial practices and traditions. *Where* allows us to not only be more specific in our research, but to acknowledge whether a particular work will resonate or benefit us. For example, I most likely would not benefit from a work written by someone in North Italy, since my family hails from Calabria. I would, however, be benefitted by reading a work by a Southern Italian practitioner or a research paper that focuses on the Calabrese region.

HOW?

How was the information in this paper/book gathered? How is the information presented?

How this helps us:

How information is gathered follows on from *when, what,* and *who* in allowing us to more extensively study and become familiar with the way in which information is gathered and presented in a work. This may include a particular academic approach, a visit to a country to learn from individuals, and so on and so forth. When we study and critically think about how the information is presented, it allows us to look at whether or not this information is beneficial to us. It also allows us to understand that there may be particular biases that need to be acknowledged in order to get the full benefit of the text.

*

While some may begin their reconnection journey already within the culture, for many of us, research is the first step as we move into reconnection. Research allows us space to not only gather information about the culture, but allows us to reach out and connect to teachers, community members, and researchers who may be able to assist us with our gathering of information. Another method of research is one I instructed one of my mentees in, which actually utilizes the structure of a specific academic paper on the vernacular healing tradition in Calabria, Italy, to understand folk medicine and magic in a full context. The parameters of the paper were created in thirteen categories, which were conceptualized in 1995 by ethnographer and folklorist David Hufford. These parameters were created to learn more about complementary and alternative medicine (CAM) systems, whose boundaries are not always fixed (Krippner, Budden, Bova, Gallante, 2011). The following categories were included:

1. What are the specialized terms in the system? (Lexicon)
2. What classes of health and sickness does the system recognize and address? (Taxonomy)
3. How was the body of knowledge derived? (Epistemology)
4. What are the key mechanisms understood to be? (Theories)
5. What are the primary goals of the system? (Goals for interventions)
6. What constitutes a successful intervention? (Outcome measures)
7. Who uses and who practices the system? (Social organization)

8. What do the practitioners do? What do they use? (Specific activities)

9. What are the responsibilities of the practitioners, patients, families, and community members? (Responsibilities)

10. How extensive are the system's applications? (Scope)

11. What are the risks and costs of the system? (Analysis of benefits and barriers)

12. How does the system view suffering and death? (Views of suffering and death)

13. What does this system provide that the dominant system does not provide? How does this system interact with the dominant system? (Comparison and interaction with dominant system)

FINDING SOURCES AND CROSS-REFERENCING

Resources are a valuable addition to your reconnection journey. They aren't just academic materials and books, but also the people you choose to follow, obtain resources from, and take the classes of. In the age of the internet, it's incredibly easy to find information about certain cultures, traditions, and folk practices—but not all of it may be accurate or helpful in our reconnection journey.

When I began my path to learning about Italian American folk magic, I stumbled upon a book on Italian witchcraft. This book was the first piece of literature that popped up for me when attempting to look for sources. Within the book, there was discussion of a lot of practices including working with the Lares, ancient Roman spirits, the Italian wheel of the year, and more. Every few chapters, I would go to my mom and share things that I found interesting with her, but every time I did, she expressed confusion.

"I don't remember my grandma doing anything like that," she said. It quickly became clear to me that what was written as an ancient tradition in Italy and advertised as the true Italian witchcraft wasn't accurate for my family, so I put the book down and went back to the drawing board.

When I was asking my mom about the practices described in this book or even sharing pieces of the writing with her, I was cross-referencing the text. I was lucky enough to have someone who remembered what our familial tradition looked like, but cross-referencing is an incredibly important part of finding reliable sources. Sometimes, cross-referencing is already done for you. This can be the case with a lot of academic texts where they are peer-reviewed or read by other scholars in the same field. This isn't to say that academic texts don't have their issues; however, an anthropological, folkloric, or ethnographic study published by a graduate student or a well-known scholar will most likely be approaching the material through a particular lens to remove bias, have informants, and work to prove a thesis. Many of my greatest resources are ethnographic studies on folk medicine and belief in certain areas of Italy.

Cross-referencing is important for several reasons. Primarily, it allows you to fact-check or look and see if something that is written is a personal gnosis or conclusion or a piece of the beliefs, culture, and magic of the community you are working to reconnect to. If you are reading a book that is stating that a particular area of Italy has continued to be pagan or has underground witch-cults into the modern day, while another book by an author born in that region is discussing how the practices are syncretized with Catholicism, you may have a problem. Cross-referencing also allows you to look at themes within belief and culture throughout a large region while recognizing smaller, more regional differences between communities. In Italy, bioregion plays a huge role in the type of plants that are used in folk healing and medicine for the people, but there are several plants that grow across a large expanse of the country—leading to that plant being found in multiple regional prayers, healing methods, and beliefs. Finally, cross-referencing allows you to look at people you are hoping to learn from and figure out if they are sharing accurate information about the culture you are working to reconnect with. Is the information they shared about this community and culture accurate to the research you have done and what other people are saying? Do the majority of the community agree that this is common sentiment or a regional, tribal, or geological difference of belief? Or are the majority of well-known practitioners in your community writing articles, making videos, and more discussing how this is not accurate or found in their practice and community?

Cross-referencing is one aspect of the research process that allows you to utilize critical thinking when engaging with books and media. Eventually, you'll begin to notice patterns between books and creators sharing similar information—like many well-known Italian American folk practitioners, writers, and creators, who share similar herbs that are important within the tradition or folk belief. This helps you not only to choose reliable and trustworthy books and individuals to engage with and learn from, but to build a knowledge base that extends past what your immediate community has to offer.

While academic sources are incredibly helpful to those on their reconnection journey, they aren't always easy to access. Sites like JSTOR often put academic articles behind a paywall, while the ones available may not be the exact ones you need. Furthermore, hard copies of scholarly and peer-reviewed texts can cost anywhere in the $20–100 range, depending on the availability, and may not even be translated into your first language. Many of my friends who are fellow reconnectors have run into the issue of finding the perfect paper in a different language, behind a paywall, or inaccessible to them for various reasons. My trick is always to email the writer. While nonprofit sites like JSTOR do pay fees to publishers, the publishers of these papers may not pay the authors, researchers, or even editors of the academic research and you may have luck in receiving a copy of the paper for free from them by just expressing interest. In a perfect world, knowledge like this would be free—the book that I am writing would be free. Many writers are continuing to work to make their content and research accessible in the face of a system that demands time, labor, and money for learning, and by working to provide each other with methods of accessing knowledge, we are working to help each other expand our knowledge and learn—without paying large corporations for it. Finding resources is not just about cross-referencing and identifying reliable sources, but reaching out to the community around you to assist you in accessing them.

Cross-referencing not only allows you to determine reliable information, but pushes you to learn from a variety of sources and to draw your own conclusions. This practice remains imperative, because it's easy for a practitioner to learn a tradition, custom, or ritual from someone else and remove the cultural context and/or original source for it—even going so far as to pass it off as something else. This can and will turn from the appreciation of a culture and its folk medicine into the appropriation of it. By double checking our sources and cross-referencing, we are able to find accurate information around our own traditions and culture we are working to reconnect to while also maintaining a healthy respect and boundary around traditions and culture that are not ours.

Part of accountable reconnection is not only working to connect with your ancestors' culture, but understanding how it fits in your identity. In their three-part documentary series, *Race: The Power of an Illusion*, California Newsreel utilizes several different perspectives when talking about the difference between race, nationality, ethnicity, and culture. When we are understanding what race is, it's imperative to understand that race is "socially imposed and hierarchal", explains Dalton Conley, a sociologist interviewed for the series. He goes on to say, "You can only have one race, while you can claim multiple ethnic affiliations. You can identify ethnically as Irish and Polish, but you have to be essentially either Black or white . . . There is an inequality built into the system. Furthermore, you have no control over your race; it's how you are perceived by others" (California Newsreel, 2003).

According to John Cheng, a historian and associate professor of Asian and Asian American studies at Birmingham University who was also interviewed, "Ethnicity isn't just a question of affiliation; it's also a question of choice. It's also a question of group membership . . . It's also often confused or conflated with nationality, but that's not the same thing. Today people identify with ethnicity positively because they see themselves as being part of that group. People can't just simply say, 'Well, I want to become a member of that race.' You either are or are not a member of that race. Whereas, if you wanted to look at ethnicity based on culture, you could learn a language, you can learn a custom—there are things that you can learn so that you could belong to that group" (California Newsreel, 2003).

Also interviewed was David Freund, historian and author of *Colored Property*, who reminds us that "both ethnic and racial identities have changed a lot throughout history," discussing the experiences of Italians, Jews, and Slavs who were "considered non-white in popular political discourse of the late nineteenth and early twentieth centuries, and this discourse grew very influential in the anti-immigration movement, leading eventually, in the 1920s, to severe restrictions against entry of supposedly non-white groups to this country ... Most of these immigrants were not running around in the nineteenth and early twentieth centuries, proudly announcing that they're Italian Americans or Slavic-Americans because at the time, it was often very dangerous and at least a disadvantage to be identified that way" (California Newsreel, 2003).

Sumi Cho, a legal scholar and professor of law at DePaul University, also raised a very important point, telling California Newsreel, "In the law, I think there's a failure to seriously grasp the significance of the impact of racial exclusion and white supremacy in this society. There are many who don't believe that racial divisions are much different from ethnicity-based divisions; i.e., what African Americans have faced in this country is little different from what Irish Americans or Italian Americans have faced ... There's an asymmetry that's important to keep in mind when we're talking about race versus ethnicity" (California Newsreel, 2003).

Nationality, distinct from ethnicity and race, represents "the status of belonging to a particular nation, whether by birth or naturalization" (Dictionary.com), and culture is even more nuanced. Zaretta Hammond, teacher and author of *Culturally Responsive Teaching and the Brain*, created a visual known as the "culture tree" to help us more fully understand the ways in which it operates, presents, and even transforms.

The culture tree contains: areas of surface culture, such as observable elements like music; then shallow culture, including social interactions, rules about interaction like eye contact and touching; and finally deep culture, which includes unconscious assumptions, governing world views, and cosmology surrounding health, ethics, and even spirituality.

Deep culture exists at the roots—it is our group identity, world view, relationships to nature and animals, spirituality, and concepts of self. It influences our notions of fairness and decision-making. These roots feed our shallow culture, the trunk—our concepts of time, food sources, theories of wellness and disease, child rearing, ways of handling emotion and more. The trunk feeds our leaves, or surface culture—our music, art, language, cooking, styles of talking, holidays, clothes and more. Each element of culture relies on the culture next to it, and each is influenced by various factors.

I was raised in America—to an extent, my culture is influenced by this nationality and socially acceptable culture patterns. I was also raised in a family with Italian-immigrant ancestors—who held certain behaviors of culture and passed them down to me through generations. Together, they blended together and created who I am. Being of Italian descent does not give me access to the culture my ancestors were a part of, because I am not active within that culture—I have to work to understand it and become part of it. Even a disconnect from Italian American culture requires me to reconnect. I may be aware of some elements of surface culture, such as food, language, and music, but may not have access to shallow or deep culture at the beginning of my reconnection journey due to generational drift.

It's also important to note that "ancestry" is not the same as national identity. "Italian" is a nationality, but not an ancestry, nor is it a race. The white racialization of Italians can be argued to be political. Many Italian Americans have genetic ancestry that comes from North Africa and the Middle East. Within this, many different terms non-exclusive to "Italian American" could be referring to someone's ancestry, national identity, or ethnicity depending on how they define the different terms.

If you feel like none of these give you a solid answer to what culture, nationality, race, or even ethnicity is—it's because each section of these identities is fluid, changing, and growing even as you read this. Race and "whiteness" as a social and hierarchal construct is not the same now as it was a hundred or even fifty years ago. Culture continues to grow, change, and adapt as the people within it adapt. Someone can be fully one race, yet be raised within the culture of a specific ethnic group and fully identify with that culture. Reconnection is messy, it is personal, and it exists in an in-between place for many people. The experience I have as a white Italian American is different from the experience of my friend who is Roma and Sicilian and is visibly Brown, or my friend who is Italian American and Black. It is also different from that of my sister, who is ethnically Italian American yet is recognized by others as non-white. It will not be the same for my teachers, who lived in a generation where Italian Americans were still facing xenophobia and violence for continuing to keep their culture alive.

Connecting with a culture or heritage that your family has previously been disconnected from does not change your race or nationality—these remain. You cannot change the color of your skin and how others perceive you racially, or where you were born. Throughout a variety of countries, race is still a factor of identity that affects how others see you, contributing to both privilege and discrimination. Another important factor of reconnection is recognizing that you, as a reconnector, may not have faced the same struggles and discrimination as those born in the culture or ethnicity you are working to reconnect with. At the same time, being disconnected from a nationality or culture makes it so you, as a reconnector, may have different understandings of societal norms, value systems, and place in the social hierarchy due to your nationality, race, and ethnicity.

Recognizing our privileges by way of race, nationality, or even current culture allows us space to hold accountability for the ways that privilege has made our lives easier and will even make our reconnection easier. Throughout this book, you will be asked to check in on your privileges in a variety of ways—whether that's race, class, gender, or nationality. Reconnection requires this level of self-reflection and self-awareness to ensure that you don't fall into the pitfalls of problematic thinking or ideology, which tend to persist throughout reconnection and spiritual circles in a variety of ways. For more about the ways in which problematic thinking and ideology can affect your reconnection journey and what to look out for, see page 211.

CREATING BOUNDARIES AND LEARNING FROM ONLINE SPIRITUAL COMMUNITIES

Every individual practitioner will have a different comfort level for what they want to share in online spiritual communities. However, here are a few things that are absolutely not okay and can be considered red flags when seeking out community online.

SPIRITUAL BYPASSING

Spiritual bypassing is a term that refers to a tendency to utilize spirituality and spiritual practices to avoid facing emotional issues or even real-world consequences to your actions. Spiritual bypassing has extended as a term to include the social activism sphere, especially in pushing the idea that caring about other people or contributing to communities in meaningful ways is "low vibrational." This is a term that is often utilized by new age spirituality circles that indicate an inherent vibration to all things including beings, often with a moral attachment of high being "good" and "low" being bad. These ideologies also tend to run in the same circles as toxic positivity, a phenomenon and term representing a pressure to remain happy and suppress negative emotions or reactions to the world around us. Spiritual bypassing can include weaponizing a spiritual practice to claim superiority over those who don't share the same practice, avoidance of uncomfortable feelings that may arise surrounding spirituality, idealism surrounding your spiritual practice, and focusing on spirituality only but ignoring present situations, issues, and feelings. Well-known examples often arise from Christianity, such as telling someone that praying for something hard enough will fix a problem or that "everything happens for a reason." Not only does spiritual bypassing dismiss the emotions and experiences of those around us, but it can lead to our boundaries, and emotional well-being being dismissed or brushed off. The inherently harmful nature of spiritual bypassing is one that pervades online spiritual communities. The shifting of blame, and shunning those that don't fit your ideals of what spirituality should look like all represent elements of spiritual bypassing that cause real harm to individuals around you. When we enter online communities, beware of the following red flags:

✤ The belief that prayer, spells, or magic will fix issues and are all you need rather than being a tool to create change, community, and power for yourself and others

✤ The belief that one way of being and practicing is correct, and the other ways are incorrect

✤ The usage of spirituality or practice to elevate one's superiority

- ✢ The argument that certain emotions or conversations are "low vibrational" or not something that should be talked about
- ✢ The prioritizing of positivity to a point where it is harmful to the emotions and well-being of the people around you, including shutting down their emotions and experiences
- ✢ The blaming of personal faults or mistreatment of others on a celestial being or astrology
- ✢ The belief that working with or venerating a spirit passes all those qualities on to you, absolving you from any work, reflection, or accountability
- ✢ The belief that you are able to bypass initiatory rites or respectful methods of approaching a spirit or spiritual practice due to your interest in the spirit
- ✢ The belief that you are absolved from responsibility and accountability for harmful and hurtful actions towards others when they are having a difficult time

Also note that spiritual bypassing can take many forms and this list is by no means exhaustive.

RACISM, SEXISM, HOMOPHOBIA, TRANSPHOBIA, AND ABLEISM

While many people believe this goes without saying, racism, sexism, and ableism are rampant within spiritual communities. The presence of these three things presents differently, but the way in which each one "others" individuals and harms our communities is prevalent and insidious. While some instances of racism are well-known, others can easily permeate reconnection spaces. In the words of renowned philosopher, author, and political activist Angela Y. Davis, "In a racist society, it is not enough to be non-racist, we must be anti-racist" and this holds true within spiritual spaces. Seeking counsel only from folks within your tradition, and brushing aside racism within your community spaces ultimately allows racism to thrive. The teachers and resources you should be referring to in conversations on anti-racism and decolonization are those that have experienced it and navigate it in their everyday. For books about anti-racism written by people of color, see page 237. In a similar vein, sexism and ableism easily co-opt spiritual spaces. Throughout the spirituality revival of the seventies, women were consistently treated as lesser and women of color even more so to the point where sexism is still ingrained and present in many different circles. Lateral violence, or displaced anger and rage that continues to be directed towards members within a minority or marginalized community rather than the oppressors of the community, is incredibly prevalent in spiritual circles. It's easy to turn against your peers or the people you feel are different to you, but in reality it's not often the people around you within your community that are doing you harm. Rather, the harm comes from institutionalized and systemic violence against your community by oppressors. A well-known, historical example of lateral violence is the case of the early suffragettes. Susan B. Anthony only fought for white women's rights. Instead of positioning herself against the oppressor and the patriarchal white supremacist structures that stood against women as a whole, Anthony chose to protect whiteness in order to get a step ahead. Historically, the year that women gained suffrage was the year white women gained suffrage, often leaving women of color, and many groups of othered individuals, on the sidelines of first-wave feminism.

Homophobia and transphobia tend to run in the same circles—the belief that someone who is gay doesn't belong within witchcraft or the idea that trans women aren't "real women" is startlingly apparent within modern witch books. There is a tendency to place power on organs such as the womb, and identifying the womb as a symbol of "womanhood" is an all-too-common sentiment that is not only transphobic, but actually excludes a variety of cis women with different life experiences, such as those who have had a hysterectomy. We also see issues of accessibility in spiritual spaces; including ideas surrounding practice and how it should be done or how frequently, and in-person spiritual events where there are no accessibility measures are taken. In some spiritual and religious spaces, disabilities are considered to be karmic, meaning that something was done in a previous life to deserve a disability in this life—or even that the disabled person "chose" their life before birth. Not only does this perpetuate a problematic idea that someone with a disability is deserving of their difficult experiences, but it ultimately dismisses the fact that we also have the capability to live joyful, fulfilled lives.

Anti-medication and anti-vaccination sentiments are prevalent in some spiritual circles, creating dangerous environments for disabled people and anyone with a compromised immune system. These issues may be easily ignored or brushed over, but a few things can be looked at to give you more information about a spiritual person and their space:

✢ Who do they associate with? Are those individuals trustworthy and kind?

✢ What is the relationship to the community they're in, if any? If they are in a community, is it primarily individuals within positions of power in society? Are those people in the positions of power aware of it and working to uplift individuals?

✟ When receiving critique, are they automatically defensive or closed off to certain types of individuals or critique? Will they enforce the fact that they are not what they are described as and go to lengths to show it, oftentimes putting the individual who critiqued them in a position where they could be ridiculed or harassed, especially if they are a minority?

CULT MENTALITY

Several different types of cults exist, but what makes a cult a cult? Rather than a religious movement, a cult is a social phenomenon centered around an incredibly charismatic, self-appointed leader who creates a high-control environment, requiring devotion and unwavering belief and trust. In cult settings, *Discover* magazine writes, "critical thinking is often frowned upon, while absolute faith is rewarded. Guilt, shame and fear are also constantly wielded to slowly strip away an individual's identity. Free thinking, free will, and free speech are limited in an environment where full obedience to leaders is required" (Shane, 2022). While not all cults are religious or spiritual, many cults throughout history have operated through a particular spiritual belief or religious framework. Modern spiritual spaces are no different, and online communities are especially rampant with cults and cult-mentality. Certain red flags are prevalent in cult settings, and they can include the following:

✟ High control and demand, including but not limited to financial control, control of resources and possessions, and demanding attention and time

✢ Questions are met with hostility, especially surrounding practices of the group and especially when asked by "outsiders"

✢ Fear-mongering, or the leader intentionally trying to make others fear something

✢ Isolation, or the leader requiring explicit devotion as well as separation from loved ones and the outside world

✢ Us vs them mentality, which tends to harbor and push the cult as a whole, including viewing individuals outside of the cult as "lesser than," giving space for racism, homophobia, and misogyny

BULLYING, OSTRACIZING, AND SHAMING

This section, similar to the last, looks at the ways in which someone doesn't necessarily have to fit into any of the prior or future categories to treat people harmfully or hurtfully. While the way in which bullying and negativity foster themselves online looks incredibly different to the textbook definition of "bullying" we have gotten used to in primary school, it remains the same in a plethora of ways. Those who target, ostracize, and shame individuals for virtually no reason, create spaces for hatred with room to pick on others, and allow real and tangible harm to come to innocent people. It's incredibly easy for people in positions of power in society to gain larger followings on social media due to privilege, and how this privilege is utilized says a lot about the type of person they are. There's no one kind of bullying or shaming that occurs online, so in this section I'll provide a few red flags and a few questions to prompt around the people you engage with on the internet.

- Does this individual make you feel comfortable? Do they respond well to valid criticism, well-meaning comments, and/or peers?

- Does this individual have firm boundaries that they uphold? Are they respectful when talking about peers and fellow individuals?

- When something upsets this individual, do they utilize a mob mentality to go after the person who upset them? Do they respond publicly and loudly to this upset, including identifying who they disagree with/who upset them and opening up this person to harassment?

- Does this individual consistently start arguments with others for no apparent reason?

- When talking to other people about this individual, do you notice that many others have had bad experiences or felt uncomfortable, shamed by, or harassed by this individual? What is their history within the community they are a part of, and how do others think about them? In other words—is there a pattern of behavior that is harmful to others, including a behavior of bullying?

- Is this individual eager to position themselves as "better than" someone else for a variety of reasons?

- Does the individual openly exclude people for a variety of reasons?

CLASSISM

When we look at classism in the context of spirituality, it's not only looking at individuals within different class groups, but also looking at the materials they use and the methods with which they practice. It's easy to fall into the idea, especially in online spaces, that more is better and that you need specific items to complete a spell. And while certain ingredients or methods of practicing may be traditional within your context, we may not always have access to them. Classism expands beyond frowning upon individuals who you define as "less than" based on the income they receive or the way they dress, and goes into a further conversation on the way we believe we should practice witchcraft. We must remember that while one person may prioritize crystals, books, and tools with the witchy "aesthetic," this doesn't automatically make their practice better.

Consumer culture tells you that you need a specific crystal or candle to be happy and complete this or that spell, while folk belief and folk magic ask you what you have on hand to make a difference in your life right now. While we live in a society that continues to be capitalist, we can recognize the ways in which it has programmed us to consume more and feel like we are not enough as reconnectors and practitioners unless we have that specific thing. Recognizing this then allows us to deconstruct and revisit our beliefs about our practices and what we feel like we "need" in our lives to prioritize accessible materials, necessity, and community.

We also need to recognize that the certain reality of our society is that we often have to monetize our work and our time in order to survive. For many, this is our spiritual work or products, while for others this may be a job they do to make ends meet, or both. The belief that spiritual work, products, and knowledge should be free is a common one, and while it can easily fall in line with our ancestors' way of being and passing knowledge throughout community orally, it isn't necessarily historically accurate. There have always been teachers and healers that received payment for their work; however, the payment may not have been actual financial compensation, but a trade of goods, fresh food, and such. Some healers and practitioners flourished and functioned as the go-to individual within their community for healing and were often supported by the community as payment. They knew they would be safe financially, have food to eat, and receive what they needed if things got tough.

We are not currently living in our ancestors' time or community. While we may, over time, create a community that we know would support us, the current version of payment for spiritual work and products is that which will ensure our survival—financial support. When we are finding individual teachers, peers, and community through the internet, we often don't have the means to show up at their home with a meal or ensure they would have a place to go if they were out in the cold. What we can ensure, however, is that they would have the financial means to support themselves if that did happen. If we are unable to show up financially, there are many other ways to support the people we want to learn from. Recommendations of their services, sharing their public content, subscribing to newsletters, engaging with the work they offer for free and sharing it with others are all fantastic ways to support healers, practitioners, and teachers. We don't live in the communities our ancestors did and the current economic climate is more inflated and demanding than ever—something our predecessors may not have ever seen. Recognize that where we are right now and the financial and social demands we have to meet may not have ever existed for our ancestors. Considering this often gives me a different perspective around supporting the work of my spiritual and cultural teachers and peers. I know that if I am unable to show up for them physically, I can still provide financially, or recommend their content, or engage with their work in other ways that are accessible. This, in turn, allows me to recognize and release any guilt I may hold about having to charge for work and labor that historically may have been free in a community.

PART 1

HISTORY AND HOMELAND

After thinking through your intentions and moving through the different ideas pushing you to reconnect with your heritage, it's time to learn more about you and your history. This is simultaneously the most difficult and most exciting part of the journey—it is where you will have moments of "Eureka!" as well as moments where you feel as though you are more lost than you were when you started. The history of you, as a practitioner and a person, is a sum of many parts including: your homeland, the folk you are connected to, the plants, environment, and animals you are connected to, and the history of the place your ancestors are from itself. Each step allows you to understand a wider picture of who you are now based on what your history is.

HOMELAND

Learning about your homeland is going to look different for everyone who reads this book—there are those who have never set foot in their ancestors' country, those who will have difficulty sourcing what that country even is, those who spent time growing up in that country and visiting frequently, and everything in between. For those of us part of a diaspora with ancestors that left the homeland a few generations back, there's a good chance you only heard murmurs about the Old Country and instead spent most of your childhood focusing on the land you lived in. Recognizing homeland isn't about working to fit back into a puzzle that no longer fits you—your family, your ancestors, and even you have been changed by your current nationality, culture, and other environmental influences. Rather, recognizing the homeland of your ancestors is about reconnecting with the past while also looking to the future.

I will never be Italian—I will always be an Italian American, but learning about Italy, Calabria, and the town my *bisnonna* and *bisnonno* are from, allows me to learn more about the culture, beliefs, and customs that have been diluted and lost from the time my ancestors resided in Italy. It allows me to connect with not only other people who have similar ancestry and stories, but ancestral plant and animal allies that can assist me in my reconnection.

Learning about homeland can occur through a few methods—tracing family lineages and family trees, talking to family members, and utilizing public resources. In some cases, learning about particular customs and cultural beliefs can be specific to particular regions, tribes, or towns—thus creating further difficulty in narrowing the search. In some cases, the history of a lineage or family isn't publicly expressed or documented—rather, individuals or groups have done everything they can to erase it. Depending on your family's heritage, what part of the diaspora you live in, and more, it may be easier or harder to trace lineage all the way down to region. That doesn't mean reconnecting isn't for you—rather, you may have to approach it a different way and it may take you longer to find the information you are searching for.

In many cases, your diasporic culture may contribute more to your spiritual practice, customs, and beliefs than your homeland—and that's okay. Reconnection can be, in part, reconnecting to the community around you in the diaspora as well as reconnecting to the folk from your ancestors' homeland. Nationality, culture, race, and heritage all interact with one another in different ways for every practitioner, and feeling a pull to reconnect with the diasporic traditions and culture rather than where your ancestors came from is as valid an approach as any.

So what benefits are there to learning about your ancestors' homeland? How do you discover the country they came from and more about it? Recognizing the region and area of your heritage, whether this is a bioregion, tribal land, or recognized country allows you to more fully understand and learn about your ancestors including how they lived, what was important to them, and even beliefs and customs tied to the land. Through learning the history, before you even begin to reconnect with your plant and animal ancestors, you can know about the folk magic and traditions from where your ancestors came from. Were they from a rural, farming town? Did they live high up in mountains near old, sacred sites? What churches, temples, or landmarks were near them? Are there certain legends or traditions associated with their country or region of origin? Did they frequent any churches, temples or landmarks to participate in devotional activities? Which spirits, saints, or deities were they stewards of?

To help you get started, here are a few things that you can do to begin researching your homeland and practical steps you can take to tackle this task:

1. Begin researching on a genealogy site. Talk to your relatives for names that you can use to begin the process of building a family tree. Research your family lineage as far back as you can, gathering different names, places of origin, and more. See if they know the nation or region that your ancestors came from and, if not, see if the family tree allows you to reach back far enough to find the nation. Make sure you heavily research the site you are planning to use, as some tend to sell information or are run by organizations you may not want to support.

2. If you know or are able to find the nation that your ancestors came from, begin to look for articles—both academic and non-academic—that discuss the superstitions, beliefs, and customs that are part of your homeland. This can include holidays, festivals, spiritual beliefs, major religions, and current and past political history.

3. If you know or are able to find the region that your ancestors came from, begin to look for more specific

articles discussing customs, and important holidays centered around your region. See if this region has similarity to nation-wide holidays, festivals, and beliefs and which ones stick out as being confined to the region or holding more importance in the region.

4. After looking at major holidays, customs, and festivals, expand your search into folkloric traditions and folk beliefs associated with the region of your homeland. You can also ask your family about this. The best way that I've found of doing this is not to ask about "magic" or "witchcraft," but to ask what family members did in certain situations. What was done when someone was having bad luck? Were there any days of the year that specific meals or foods were made? Were there certain ideas or superstitions that were wide-held in the nation or region? Was something done to help someone with luck, finding a husband, or to make the crops grow? Recognize religion and spiritual ways of being as a lifeway or a method of existing rather than a system.

5. Once you understand the folkloric traditions and beliefs a little more, you can begin to look into sacred sites, temples, churches, and more in the region of your ancestors. This will help you learn more about the local spirits, deities, and saints that your ancestors would have worshipped or worked with. In Italy, the folk beliefs and spirituality have been heavily syncretized with Catholicism, including some temples to saints and apparitions of Mary, which were originally deity temples of ancient Roman or Greek origin (Blunt, 1823). Understanding what sacred sites and temples are within your ancestors' region will allow you to further

understand past spiritual beliefs and entities that your ancestors are tied to and you may be interested in connecting with.

6. Spend some time researching your ancestors' bioregion. Bioregion refers to an area defined by characteristics of the natural environment rather than by man-made divisions, often seen in major ecological biomes. Some examples of a bioregion could be an area defined by ridges, peaks, trenches, or other topographical landmarks. For example, if your ancestors came from a very mountainous land, it is likely they worked with more mountain spirits, as well as the flora and fauna that naturally occur on mountains. Understanding bioregion allows you to connect with your ancestors by understanding what regional landmarks they saw every day, what native plants grew in their environment that may have influenced folk medicine, cuisine, and apotropaic charms, as well as understanding what kind of life they led. Did they live in a fertile valley where farming was easy, or did they struggle to make the crops grow each year?

Note that when we reconnect, two different things are occurring—we are reconnecting with our ancestors and we are reconnecting with our ancestral cultures. The former is not necessarily a reconnection with ancestral culture, rather reconnecting with the people, their stories, and how they led us to where we are now. The latter is different, requiring acculturation, and is far more difficult when we no longer have access to the culture.

Each of these research steps will help you to learn more about where your ancestors came from and what exactly that means for you as a reconnector. As you begin to get a bigger picture, you may feel pulled to take action in one way or another to connect with your ancestors' homeland on a deeper level. Below you'll find a scale/gradient of least to most expensive ways of furthering this connection with your ancestors' homeland.

Accessible right now:
When your budget is limited, it may feel like reconnection is out of the picture for you. However, even going to your local library and searching for resources regarding history, language, and more allows you to learn about your ancestors' homeland while also being in a quiet setting that is close to your home. If you attend college or high school, your school most likely has a library that is free for you to use and may hold academic sources in the areas you seek. Learning everything you can about your ancestors' region and even seeing if your professor or teacher can help you get access to academic papers, documentaries, and more will help you become acquainted with bioregion, politics, customs, and folk beliefs of your ancestors' region. Furthermore, embodying reconnection, creating a somatic link, embodying this work is foundational and accessible to everyone. To decide to reconnect and embrace an ancestral link, hold space for the ancestral memory and what has been passed to you, is what colors our reconnection journey. To begin it is to recognize it, to hold space for it, to hold your body's memory and the ancestor you currently are as paramount as you move forward.

Middle ground:
Take some time to research local communities that hold some form of your culture or are similar to your ancestors' homeland. This emphasizes connection with the folk you

are working to reconnect with while also allowing you some leniency in budget. There may be a local market nearby that emphasizes the food and cuisine of your ancestors' culture, a center for those from your heritage, or even a museum or learning center that allows reconnectors to learn more in person. As the middle ground, you can expect to pay for travel fees, but this task is limited in accessibility for those who have difficulty driving/transporting themselves, have sensory issues that limit their ability to go to new places, or those who have no form of community near them.

Investment:

Visit your ancestors' homeland! Visiting where your heritage comes from is one of the most expensive ways to connect with your ancestors. It allows you to explore the bioregion and sacred sites, learn their language through lived experience, and more. This, however, is not the most accessible option. A pilgrimage can be expensive, and not everyone will know the exact region their ancestors came from. Additionally, depending on the nation, there may be difficulties in accessibility.

HISTORY

Your reconnection journey is influenced by many things, including the folk, plant allies, and animals, but it begins with learning your history. This could be the history of the region of your ancestors or the history of the diaspora you are working to reconnect with. History means a couple of things—in a technical sense, it is the study of past events. In a reconnection journey, learning your history also means history that may not be documented in history books—this could include oral traditions or even the entirety of the history of your people that is painted in an accurate light. All too frequently, textbooks and sources tend to paint a particular picture of historical events, especially when pertaining to minorities and people of color and their history. We see this frequently on Turtle Island (North America) with the way Thanksgiving is taught, specifically that the European colonizers were kind to the Indigenous dwellers, when the opposite was true. Similar occurrences happen all over the world—those in power have the ability to paint a picture however they want, and minorities are often those that are shirked in the writing.

The importance of learning history comes into play here. Not just the textbooks, but what is spoken and told by the folk. Oral traditions and listening to the people allows you to learn from them firsthand. When we learn from the people, we don't just get to learn their side of history, but also the medicines, folklore, superstitions, and beliefs that inform their experiences and the way they live. What is central to their belief system? What do they value? How does this inform their experiences and what they do? Learning the history of the people allows you to engage further with community, understand the root of beliefs and ideas, or begin to recognize them, and helps you further the understanding that the folk are not a monolith. In certain countries, like Italy, folk beliefs and medicines change between the different regions. When we look at Italy's map and history, we can see that Italy was not what we would refer to as a papal state, but a variety of different kingdoms. Italy's history is also influenced by those who have occupied it. This includes ancient Etruscans, Italic tribes, the Roman Empire, Arabic peoples, the Celts, and even the Phoenicians depending on the region in Italy.

In the mid-nineteenth century, Giuseppe Garibaldi founded the Italian nation-state, leading to modernization and colonization of other countries in the Mediterranean as well as Africa. While this occurred, Southern Italy stayed rural and poor, creating a divide between the North and the South that would lead in part to the diaspora and immigration of Southern Italians to Turtle Island. The other aspect that contributed to mass immigration is the discrimination that occurred after the unification of Italy.

While this history is short and does not nearly encompass the different political climates, people, and history of Italia, it shows us that learning our history benefits us and contributes to our ability to understand the folk we are reconnecting with. When we talk to our elders, we are able to learn firsthand about the way in which sliding political climates, history, and more have affected the beliefs and lived experiences of the folk we are reconnecting with.

Furthermore, according to folklorists, and various other bodies of research, a heavy reliance on oral transmission is generally considered to be a definitive feature of all aspects of folk culture. This includes, but is not limited to, folk medicine, folk beliefs, and folk magic. While understanding the importance of oral traditions varies from culture to culture, folk healing traditions and recipes often have a heavier dependence on orality in passing down traditions and knowledge in contrast to other healing systems (O'Connor and Hufford, 2001).

While these recipes have changed over the years and remain different between regions and diasporic practices, Krippner et al. note that, "Recipes for protective formulae are typically passed on to younger family members on Christmas Eve or Saint John's Eve [23 January], after which time the previous practitioner stops using the procedure" (Krippner, Budden, Gallante, Bova, 2011). These elements of folk magic and medicine in Italy have continued into the diasporic traditions and are noted by several different authors of Italian heritage, such as Mary-Grace Fahrun and Agostino Taumaturgo. While this example is specific to Italian folk magic and Italian diasporic practices, the importance of oral tradition and passing down of rites, rituals, and prayer continues throughout folk beliefs and magic around the world. Your reconnecting journey may not include engaging in folk magic and practices, but learning about them, especially when they are heavily ingrained into the culture you are working to reconnect with, gives you insight into the social class, medicines, and more used by the folk.

Here are some practical steps you can take to begin learning about the history of the folk and your ancestors' homeland:

1. Begin to read academic papers, such as ethnographic, anthropological, or sociological studies targeted at the folk medicine within your ancestors' homeland. Oftentimes, the key words here will be "oral tradition," "vernacular healing tradition," or even just "folk medicine". Databases like academia.edu allow scholars and researchers to upload their works and readers to download them for free.

2. Invest in books written by folk practitioners actively within the practice. This may be more difficult to find depending on the folk magic—some folk magics have little to no information available online, such as Armenian folk magic, or they may be writings primarily by individuals who don't have the full experience of the folk magic or misrepresent it.

3. Spend time researching practitioners and teachers of the folk magic—this is a tricky step and one that needs both patience and nuance. Some teachers only operate by word of mouth while others are more open with their offerings and conduct them online. For more on community and seeking mentorship and teachers, see page 67.

4. Begin to connect with folk practitioners of the magic and culture. This can be done online or within your local area. Many of my peers who have passed knowledge on to me have been people I've met through my research, but also individuals that I've connected with on social media.

5. Seek out the authors of the books and academic papers you have read. Ask questions if they're open to it, or see if they have available workshops and lectures you can attend.

DIASPORA

When we talk about diaspora and diasporic traditions, we are talking about a term that is ever-changing in practice and academic terms. There are diasporas all over the world and some diasporas are well-known, while others are less so. Diaspora in our current day and age indicates the dispersion or spread of a people from their original homeland. This could be by force, such as the Jewish diaspora and African diaspora, or by choice to explore work or trade in a different country. Diasporic communities retain a strong attachment with their country of origin through varying ties, such as historical memory, family ties, or a sense of identity. Oftentimes displacement leads to an ever-evolving culture outside of the country of origin.

While the ties to the origin homeland may remain, culture and traditions there will continue to change, separately to how they will be changing and developing in the diaspora. Traditions and stories change as they are passed down through generations, and continue to evolve and grow in the present day. To understand the ways in which diasporas form their own cultures over time, we can look at cuisine. On Turtle Island, Italian food is typically known by a few staple dishes, including but not limited to lasagna, baked ziti, and chicken parmesan. However, one of these dishes didn't actually originate in Italy—it was created by Italian immigrants on the East Coast of Turtle Island. What we could find in Italy prior to mass immigration was *melanzane alla parmigiana,* or eggplant parmesan, whose origin is claimed by the South of Italy like Calabria, Campania, Puglia, and Sicily. While we can see similarities between the recipes for *melanzane alla parmigiana* and chicken parmesan, the latter was created within the diaspora. Another example is rotis. Rotis are made both in the Caribbean and in India, but the food sharing a name doesn't actually mean they're the same. In India, to make a roti, you roll out the dough, made with *maida* or refined wheat flour, into a thin round and cook it without any oils on a hot skillet, then over an open flame till it puffs up. In the Caribbean, rotis are cooked by proofing the dough, making rounds, rolling them out, adding a fat, then rolling them back up to create layers. They are cooked on a skillet with fat to make them crispy, and some regions will also smash them together to loosen the layers. This food has the same name, but diasporic changes due to availability of ingredients, regional cooking differences, and time have created two different things.

Cuisine is just one of the many aspects of the way diasporic communities evolve and grow over time, completely separate from the country of origin's culture and changes. Politics, beliefs, necessity, availability, and more contribute to diasporic culture and traditions. Diasporas may not come from one country of origin or a unified country, but many different locations and places. What unites a diasporic community is cultural and/or ethnic background, but understanding the way diaspora functions for different communities allows us to approach reconnection in the way that will work for each of us on a personal level. Reconnection is required across time and space, including understanding where a group of individuals were and at what time. An example of this is the Jewish diaspora—the Jewish diaspora is defined as those who have not one place of origin, but many. Jewish individuals could come from Germany, Iran, Italy, or more and have had to flee due to persecution. The Jewish diaspora is primarily classified by the distinct regional groups that existed during the Middle Ages due to dispersion and resettlement. Ashkenazic Jews refers to the diasporic community that settled along the Rhine of Western Germany and Southern France specifically during the Middle Ages. Sephardic Jews refers to the diasporic community that established itself in Iberia (Spain, Portugal, North Africa, and the Middle East). Further diasporic communities include Mizrahi, Yemenite, and Karaite Jews. In the modern day, terms to explain the Jewish diaspora have continued to evolve, while someone who is Jewish may personally identify with a country of origin, such as Germany, that is more recent than the one their ancestors immigrated from.

On the other hand, the Italian diaspora includes different continents and nationalities that are used for identification, such as Italians of Ethiopia, Italian Southern Africans, Italian Americans, Italian Canadians, Italian Australians, and more. Like other diasporas, the Italian diaspora has a shared cultural and ethnic background, but all of these diasporic communities have different cultures, traditions, and cuisines that have evolved within the country they immigrated to. Every one of these communities carries some aspect of the traditions of their country of origin with them, but each of these traditions has changed over time and through other means.

Through the immigration process and the following months, years, or even decades that a group of people continued to live within a country, separate to their ancestors' country of origin, parts of their diasporic culture changed. Italian Americans and Italian Canadians of today may be more comfortable practicing paganism and intertwining it with their folk magic rather than the Catholicism of their great-grandmother. It may be easier to cook certain diasporic dishes rather than ones from their homeland due to the availability of ingredients. The members of the diaspora may not be able to speak their ancestors' language, but may know certain traditions and aspects of the culture that have remained within their family, passed down throughout generations.

Thus, we can see how diasporic communities and cultures vary from the culture of the homeland. Reconnection to a culture oftentimes includes or may very well be limited to the diasporic community and the culture that has evolved within it. For many of us, it may be incredibly difficult to fully connect to the homeland of our ancestors merely because it has changed so much from what we were taught by our forebears. However, reconnection allows us to understand not only the diasporic culture, but the culture our ancestors came from. We can explore the language, the community, and the bioregion in a way that our ancestors would have. While we may never be assimilated fully into our homelands, as we are always affected by our diasporas and countries of birth, understanding and learning about a variety of things from our country of origin can help us reconnect and is just as important in our reconnection journey as other areas in this book.

Diaspora

(definition): the dispersion or spread of a people from their original homeland.

The historical Jewish experience gives another definition: "forced expulsion and dispersal, persecution, a sense of loss, and a vision of return." However, over the past decade, "'diaspora' has become a term of self-identification among many varied groups who migrated or whose forebears migrated from one place to another or to several other places" (Vertovec, 2005). Many self-described diasporas do not emphasize some of the same aspects associated with Jewish, African, or Armenian diasporas, rather "they celebrate a cultural creative, socially dynamic, and often romantic meaning." Understanding diaspora, a word of Greek origin meaning "to sow over or scatter," means understanding that even academics across varying disciplines disagree on the modern definition of "diaspora" and all it contains. Anthropologist Steven Vertovec argues that, "Belonging to a diaspora entails a consciousness of, or emotional attachment to, commonly claimed origins and cultural attributes associated with them. Such origins and attributes may emphasize ethno-linguistic, regional, religious, national, or other features. Concerns for homeland developments and the plight of co-members of the diaspora in other parts of the world flow from this . . . emotional attachment," while also noting that "just 'how ethnic' one is does not affect whether and to what extent someone might feel themselves part of a diaspora" (Vertovec, 2005). The Migration Data Portal refers to features of a diaspora containing migration from a country of origin in search of work, trade, or to escape conflict or persecution, an idealized, collective memory and/or myth about the ancestral home, a continuing connection to a country of origin, a strong group consciousness, and a sense of kinship with diaspora members in other countries, defining diaspora as "migrants or descendants of migrants, whose identity and sense of belonging have been shaped by their migration experience and background" (Migration Data Portal, 2020).

The meaning of diaspora is wide and varied—it has no set definition as it changes over time. While originally it was used to discuss forced displacement, such as when referring to the Jewish and African diasporas, it has become a term used by many to describe a kinship or connection with a homeland for those that live outside of it. Diaspora is not just defined by first-generation immigrants, but by foreign-born children of first-generation migrants who maintain links to their parents' home country—whether that is cultural, linguistic, historical, religious or affective (Migration Data Portal, 2020). Reconnectors and those seeking to reconnect may not be an active part of the diaspora, rather they may be looking to connect with it as well as the homeland. There may be fragments of diasporic culture and tradition, but no community. There may be cultural and historical links, but no linguistic or religious connections.

PART 2

THE FOLK AND FINDING COMMUNITY

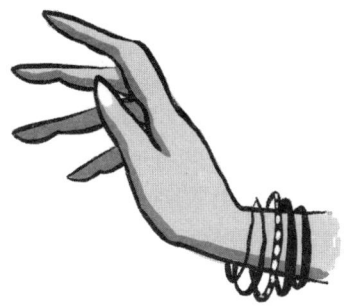

Throughout this book, you'll hear me refer to the folk. Who are the folk? They are the people of the ancestry and/or culture you are reconnecting to. They are the source of folklore, beliefs, superstitions, culture, and diasporic culture. The folk are those who create community, pass down tradition, and help us understand more about the culture we are reconnecting to. The folk are mentors, teachers, community leaders, and elders, but they are also our peers and friends. The folk are the origin for our folk practices. They allow us to learn, build community, and help us in our reconnection journey. In many reconnection journeys, we find that traditions are orally passed down—changing hands and sometimes even changing methods by being passed down from people to people.

WHO ARE THE FOLK?

While learning about your homeland may give you some ideas about culture, customs, and beliefs that are part of your heritage, the best way to understand this is to connect with the people who are reconnecting, already connected, or active within the homeland of your ancestors. Connecting with and learning from peers, mentors, and friends who are part of your ancestors' homeland allows you to expand your knowledge of the culture you are reconnecting with, trade stories, customs, and beliefs, and more.

Within my reconnection journey, I've had quite a few teachers and friends that have helped me in ways that I never expected. My first teacher, Austin, helped me recognize Diana, the Italic and Roman goddess of hunting, wild animals, women, the enslaved, and the moon as my patron and set me on the path to becoming an Italian American folk practitioner. My second teacher, Lisa Fazio, owner of the Root Circle, holds classes to connect with Italian American herbal allies. It is within her courses that I found some of my strongest ancestral plant allies and began to lean more into incorporating them in my work. I read works by Sabina Magliocco, Angela Puca, and Ernesto de Martino. I had the chance to talk with Dr Puca over video call and ask her questions about her work. Over time, I found more people online who were reconnecting to Italian folk magic or who were raised in it that I was able to learn from, share resources with, and more. Slowly, over three years of studying, discussing, and taking classes, I have found a community of folk.

While the Italian American community where I am is small, that won't be the case for everyone—pockets of people from differing backgrounds, learning and resource centers, and more exist all over the world to assist in helping people that are part of a diaspora reconnect with their culture. Learning the customs and culture firsthand can happen by reading work by writers from the cultural background you are reconnecting to, online in private communities, or via interviews either found online/in academic resources or even conducted directly with the individual. In the modern age, we have access to unlimited resources and information that our ancestors before us did not—their community was regional, based on towns, villages, and tribes set in specific areas. While our community building is different in the time of technology, intentionally connecting with and building community with the folk is an important part of your reconnecting journey.

Here are some practical steps you can take to begin communing with the folk you are working to reconnect with:

1. Ask your family about customs and culture that you may begin to reconnect with. Depending on your comfort level, you can ask anyone from a grandparent to a parent to an aunt, uncle, or cousin. Sometimes it may take a while for a family member to remember what traditions were done at Christmastime or the legends their grandparents told them, but that's okay. Patience is key in this process.

2. Research into your local community and see if there are resource or learning centers nearby. This could be a

local reservation, a community center, or even an online community or public figures that you could connect with or follow to learn more. Depending on which aspects of community customs you are interested in learning, different communities may be more beneficial to you. For example, finding a folk magic practitioner online who is connected to the culture may make more sense in your journey than attending meetings of an organization that does not offer resources to learn more about customs.

3. Learning about the folk requires learning about spiritual leaders or leaders in the community. Who is revered as a source of knowledge? Who is an elder? Depending on the culture you are reconnecting to, a spiritual leader or elder may be a tribe leader, a local rabbi, a well-revered source in the literature on the culture, or even someone in your family who knows more about the culture than you do. Spiritual leaders are typically appointed, such as priests and priestesses, by a group of people or they earn their place through years. The term "elder," on the other hand, could represent someone within the culture you are reconnecting to that is older than you and holds more knowledge than you do. Either can be approached to learn from in this situation, but respect is key when communing with your leaders and elders.

4. Finally, when reconnecting to the folk it's important to have an understanding of stigma surrounding the culture. Depending on your race, there's a good chance you are already incredibly familiar with the stereotypes and stigma that people pin on you. Identifying the stigma or stereotypes associated with your heritage and culture allows you to avoid the pitfalls of making generalizations

in your reconnection journey or stereotyping the folk you are working to reconnect with. While you may argue that you would not do this, it's easier than you think to hold unconscious biases or beliefs about your own culture and folk, especially if you're disconnected from them. Accountable reconnection requires you to look at what stigmas you already hold and believe internally so that you can work to deconstruct them. Recognize that your lineage, your heritage, is not a monolith—it is a vast community full of different people with different experiences due to environment, class, and more.

These steps will assist you in beginning your reconnection journey to the community and the folk you are working to learn from and commune with. If you are wanting to take next steps, here is another scale that allows you to look at the different ways of connecting with your community.

Accessible right now:
Community can be found in unexpected and extraordinary ways. The least expensive option for finding such is through online spaces, such as social media. This could take the place of following creators, artists, and writers; this can also be looking to see if online communities like a Discord server exist for the culture you are working to connect with. While the internet has a plethora of knowledge and is often the central way we meet and interact with individuals in this day and age, I implore you to cross-reference, fact-check, and take all information with a grain of salt. The prevalence of individuals who perpetuate harmful narratives and misinformation on the internet is vast, and it's better to find truth through multiple people or sources rather than one singular person or

online space. While these communities can sometimes have a paywall for entrance or are protected, this option is often less expensive than taking classes or traveling to local community centers. For example, I am a member of a few online communities that explore Italian American reconnection, heritage, and folk practices; one of the communities is purely to connect with and follow other teachers and creators in this sphere, while another is a Patreon that one of my favourite creators has made to learn, grow and connect. Always use caution and heavily research online communities—internet safety is an incredibly important aspect of this option. Know your boundaries, your comfort levels, and what is and isn't okay for online communities and creators you follow.

Middle ground:
To connect with your folk, use tip #2 to find resources and centers in your local community to connect with. As the middle ground option, you can expect to experience some transportation costs depending on how close this community is (bus fare, train ticket, gas for vehicle), but not nearly as much as a pilgrimage to a nation you may or may not have housing accommodations in. You can volunteer at community or resource centers, attend events that are part of your community, and more. The middle ground option also includes identifying teachers and classes that are taught by members of your community to aid in reconnection, discuss the reconnection process, or even just to help others learn the language. Taking classes with instructors who are from the culture you are working to connect with allows you to have in-person chats with members of your community that may know more than you.

Investment:

Similar to the section on homeland, a pilgrimage or journey to where your ancestors came from or to an area where the diasporic community is more prevalent is the most expensive option. It's fantastic to be able to immerse yourself into the culture you are reconnecting with—both the folk who live in the homeland as well as those in the diaspora—but traveling is both expensive and sometimes inaccessible.

RECONNECTING TO THE PEOPLE AND CULTURE

It's important to dive further into understanding not only who the folk are, but how they influence different aspects of the culture you are reconnecting to as well as methods of reconnection. This requires us to define what culture is and how the folk affect it through different lenses. To understand the folk, we have to understand a few things—what culture is, what beliefs and traditions are, and how the people living within a culture influence it. D. Stephen Long, an American theologian and professor of ethics at SMU, discusses culture as a metaphor similar to its literal translation in the book *Theology and Culture*. He says, "Culture names the thing growing in the petri dish. But over the years, the term 'culture' shifted from a noun of a process to a 'metaphor.' This occurred when culture no longer applied to a discussion of what people did to the soil and other 'natural' phenomena and instead applied the term to what happens to people. When this occurred, culture became a metaphor" (Long, 2008). Culture is a term that everyone thinks of in a different way—depending on the method in which someone is approaching it, it will have an incredibly different definition from a separate method. In simple terms, culture is defined as "all the ways of life including arts, beliefs, and institutions of a population that are passed down from generation to generation" (LaMorte,

2016). Culture is a continuously changing term—it was originally a noun meaning "cultivation." When we understand culture as a metaphor—as how our environments, beliefs, institutions, and ideas change with us and inform us—we can begin to understand culture. The people you are working to reconnect with are directly tied to a particular culture and this particular culture contains traditions, beliefs, and practices that have been influenced not only by institutions and major movements, but the people themselves. Our sense of self, language, communication, and dress are all ways in which culture affects us—to reconnect with the folk is to reconnect with the culture that they are a part of. This may be a diasporic culture or the culture of your ancestors' homeland.

Culture as we understand it now is an umbrella term including different aspects that directly affect the folk—from how we greet each other to food, beliefs, and how we carry ourselves in a community setting. Culture affects every part of our life. Cultural differences between where you are now, as a reconnector, and those you are reconnecting to—whether that is diaspora or homeland—are among the first things to take into consideration when embarking on this journey. These can be broken down into sections and methods of reconnection that further help us connect with the folk.

One of these methods is learning the language. Some individuals working on reconnecting with culture may already speak the language of their ancestors while others may have grown up speaking something completely different. If you are lucky, your language may still be taught in schools or you may be able to access a teacher online. In certain situations, such as that of Indigenous individuals on Turtle Island, their language may be more difficult to access or may only have a few fluent speakers left. This is the result of residential schools working to eradicate Indigenous tribes and forcing them to leave behind their culture and speak English. Speaking the language of your ancestors does not just stop at being able to communicate in their native tongue or talk to elders who may not speak English—many times, resources on beliefs and culture are not available in English. Language can be one of the first steps into the culture, allowing you insight into not only the way your ancestors communicated with each other but cultural superstitions (like *tocca fero,* or the custom of touching iron to ward off bad luck) that have spread to where you are today.

Beliefs and traditions are also important aspects of culture, and both can be defined in slightly different ways. Tradition may be values, holidays and celebrations, while beliefs are things that often influence those traditions. While you may not decide to observe all of the traditions or believe all of the ideas your ancestors did, reconnecting to the folk requires you to explore and learn about these ideas as a subset of culture.

When we are reconnecting, we will often find traditions are outdated or no longer make sense in our modern context.

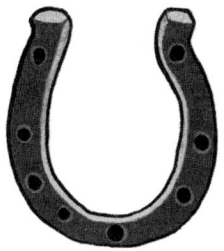

This may lead to us reconstructing a tradition in a way that will work for us right now. The most important part of this process is not the act of reconstruction, but the ability to look at an outdated or offensive tradition, understand how it functioned in the cultural context, and be able to remove the offense from it while still keeping the tradition in line with how it originally functioned.

To demonstrate this, I'm going to reference a specific divinatory method catalogued in *Italian Magic: Secret Lives of Women* by Karyn Crisis. This particular method uses a candle and seven virgins to assist someone who is petitioning Our Lady for another's health. While the individual walks to the local church to petition the Virgin Mother, seven virginal girls will pray over a candle and watch the flame to see if the petition will be successful. As the individual walks, they will look for specific signs on the roadways, such as seeing an ox, to let them know if the petition will succeed as well. To understand this particular divinatory rite, recorded in a town in Umbria, we have to understand the cultural context in which it functioned. While this book was written recently, we know that for a long time Italy has been vehemently Catholic and with these ideas of Catholicism come ideas of patriarchy. These ideas of patriarchy permeate not only this ritual, but ideas around virgin women being pure, cultural standards transferred to Italian Americans who immigrated, superstitions around pregnancy, and more. Virgins are commonly associated with "purity," "innocence," and Our Lady, Mother of God, but they also have roots pre-Catholicism in Southern Italy, meaning someone who is sovereign, currently celibate, or unmarried. We know now that the idea of virgin prayer being more innocent or pure than that of someone who has had sex, especially one who identifies as a woman, is based in ideals that fuel modern-day misogyny, despite their origins. The virgins in this practice may have been considered closer to Our Lady or their prayer more powerful because of that connection.

Knowing and understanding the way in which this ritual functions and how it is problematic, we can begin to reconstruct it in a way that still mimics the original divinatory practice to some degree while moving past the misogynistic ideas around virginity. Instead of using seven virgins to pray, you can choose seven devotees of the Virgin Mary or pray by yourself seven times over the candle after anointing yourself with oil dedicated to Our Lady. We can choose prayers and garb that pull in the power of Our Lady, wear perfume of her sacred plants, or burn a candle to her while practicing this divinatory rite. The other aspect of this ritual that is outdated, but not offensive, is the signs the individual sees while walking to the church. In my particular town, it is incredibly unlikely to see an ox or a priest on the walk to my local Catholic parish. However, it would be more likely for me to see a rabbit, crow, hawk, or a neighbor. Thus, before starting the rite, we can be intentional in saying what these signs mean before leaving the home and change them according to our current location.

This particular example is discussing something found in folk magic, but the idea of learning from the folk permeates past candle divination. It allows us to get a sense of cultural context around certain beliefs in traditions and gives us the ability to reconstruct them if need be while still being respectful of how the original rite functioned. Talking to my mother gave me an understanding of some of the cultural beliefs I wasn't raised in due to them being purposefully left behind by her as she deemed them problematic in a way that she didn't want us to experience. This doesn't mean she wasn't passing down other aspects of the culture to me, especially beliefs around jealousy, bragging, and *mal'occhio* (the evil eye); instead she picked and chose what to give to us as she raised us. This is an important understanding that contributes to the changing culture of diaspora and diasporic traditions.

Reconnection is not just a connection to the people, but a connection to the spirits of the culture and the practice (if you choose to connect with it). I always tell my friends that I wouldn't be here if my ancestors didn't drag me or I didn't actively choose to seek out teachers and peers. Reconnection, especially to the folk, is an active choice to be a forever student, be vulnerable, and accept that sometimes you will be told "no." Reconnecting to a culture that is living automatically means reconnecting to a community of people that you may disagree with or hold different beliefs from, and it requires not only patience but respect for those people past what you wish to take and learn from the culture.

SEEKING COMMUNITY AND MENTORSHIP

Community allows us to share with and be surrounded by those who are on similar journeys to us or on completely different ones. It allows us to receive constructive criticism, feedback, and information about our reconnection that we may not otherwise have access to.

Mentors and mentorship play a very specific role in this, especially for those of us who are working to reconnect with a magical practice or folk medicine. I'm often asked how I find a mentor or what is best to look out for in mentorship—and the question isn't one I necessarily know how to answer. I found many of my mentors through the internet—they had similar backgrounds to what I was interested in learning, shared information I found helpful, or created content in line with what I felt was reminiscent of or close to my practice. I didn't approach them and ask them to mentor me—rather, I found what they had available in terms of teaching or classes and took part in it. When seeking a mentor, this is important: many teachers working within the field of magic or witchcraft are doing so as full-time jobs, and while in a perfect society we would not have to pay to receive knowledge, capitalism requires many, including spiritual teachers, to ask for payment in exchange for receiving guidance and information. Many of the authors I have been interested in also offer accessible material in the form of online content creation, seminars, and posts talking about their experiences as a member of the community or in reconnection.

Certain traditions require a teacher or mentor for initiation, the passing of oral traditions, or even connecting with the spirits of the tradition. We see this in many different religions and practices, including Judaism, Santeria, and Vodoun. While some of these initiation rites are well-known, such as the transmission of a *mal'occhio* prayer on Christmas Eve, others are kept secret within the religion and are completely unknown to outsiders. Some traditions are passed almost entirely from an elder or teacher on to a younger practitioner or person. While documentation exists to discuss particular beliefs, initiation rites, or spells within the practice, there is value in seeking out a physical teacher to assist you in learning about traditions and practices. Within these traditions lie beliefs about the religion or the cultural context surrounding the practice, and this is something that isn't always included within documented texts or books. To access community is to access those that are contributing to, have been raised in, or affected by particular aspects of culture —whether that is a particular religion, belief, or practice.

Understanding the way in which knowledge is passed from individual to individual within a spiritual practice is also imperative for recognizing when someone may not be the best source of information. When considering someone as a teacher, we don't always need to look at what kind of information they are giving, but how they are giving the information and how it makes us feel. How are they approaching sharing information? Are they open about their teachers and sources? Do they take chances to privately discuss learning moments with you or correct misinformation?

What traditions do they represent and are learned in? Are these traditions initiatory, and if so, by whom were they initiated? When we look at our elders, teachers, and peers, being open about where we received our information from and by whom is more important than one may think. While information tends to spread across the internet quickly, oftentimes losing its original source, slowing down and asking to slow down is a powerful move to protect yourself and analyze where you can get reliable information.

Here are some more rules of thumb for deciding who to learn from and about what:

1. When they share information, do they only share sources that were written by them?
2. When combatting misinformation, do they approach it from the perspective of someone who wants to help you grow and learn? Are they taking the time to give sources, information, and criticism that will help you in your practice, or does it feel as though they just don't like the way you present the information?
3. Do they react badly when you ask for sources or extra information, including getting defensive or upset?
4. If they are someone who is not of the minority in the practice, are they aware of their privilege and are they uplifting those who created the practice/religion as well as its cultural origins?
5. When they collect and share information, are they citing their sources, teachers, or giving cultural context?
6. Are they open and willing to acknowledge other forms of practices and variation within culture and tradition?

7. Do they publicly and privately share not only their teachers, but who initiated them (if any), and can you find an oral or written record of this? Within certain communities, asking point-blank for their teachers is not appropriate and an oral or written record may not be found. You can however rephrase this question to ascertain their dedication to a community, such as asking:

- Which communities are they affiliated with?
- Which communities claim them?

While this doesn't nearly encompass all of the personal experiences and public experiences I've had and seen in my communities around practitioners and mentors, nor is it a definitive list, the main point to keep in mind is how this person makes you feel. I don't mean that you disagree with some of the things they say or that you get a "bad vibe" from the content they make, but rather take some time to look at how they share information and the way in which they teach. Do you just feel as though you disagree with what they're saying? Does it confront parts of you that may make you uncomfortable? Does it make you feel embarrassed, humiliated, or uneasy? Recognizing how it makes you feel and then further breaking it down to recognize whether it is because it confronted something you need to address or something you disagree with versus discomfort because of the way it was presented is imperative. Being able to discern which teachers will help us and which want to be put on an authoritative pedestal is, in many ways, us recognizing who we are, what we want in a teacher, and how best to approach it. It's the ability for us, as reconnectors, to understand our place as forever students and furthermore how we learn and which ways of teaching benefit us. There are elements of our reconnection that we can always continue to grow into, change, and learn, and then there are elements of our reconnection we cannot control or change. This self-awareness expands past us and becomes reflective of our community and the people we take with us on this journey. It allows us to explore our roots in a way that is painful, yet beneficial to how we learn and who we become as we reconnect.

Mentorship isn't just reserved for those on spiritual paths—we can learn about culture, language, and beliefs that benefit our reconnection through a variety of teachers, peers, and community members in ways that we may not always identify as mentorship. Nor is mentorship just about younger generations learning from older, but rather all generations creating an ongoing exchange between community members who all hold different generational experiences. You can learn valuable things through people around you who don't necessarily identify as mentors—these could be people in different practices, people in the same practice, people younger or even older than you with different relationships with the folk. Teachers of language and teachers of culture can be mentors to us and assist us in reconnection, allowing us insights into particular words used, ideas, connotations, or even slang that is commonly used within the culture.

Reconnecting with culture does not just mean learning and connecting to a spiritual community, but a cultural community. While we may be seeking out reconnection to a particular tradition, religion, or even deity, we cannot understand them without the cultural context they exist in. Our ancestral reconnection may overlap with cultural reconnection, but recognizing the stories, communities, and the people who brought us to where we are is imperative to our journey. To be on the path of reconnection is an undertaking that requires us to shed particular beliefs, ideas, and cultural concepts that do not benefit us or fit who we are becoming. This is particularly potent for those shedding ideas of white supremacist ideals adopted through assimilation and those learning to reconnect and rediscover a culture after colonization. When we understand the culture that we are working to reconnect with, we can understand how it influences us, as reconnectors, as well as the diaspora we are a part of.

When talking about community, I want to mention something that one of my teachers, Lisa Fazio, who runs the Root Circle, discussed in a class I took with her. There's ancestral reclamation and cultural reclamation, she explained. Our ancestors are a part of us. We have everything we need to connect to our ancestors, because they are inside us. Cultural reclamation requires us to look outside of us—to our community, our mentors, teachers, and elders, as pillars of understanding in the culture. In Italian American culture, community and family are among the most important things. Our apotropaic charms work because they are gifted. Our cures are passed from elder or teacher to younger practitioner as a way of keeping our traditions alive, but also of giving someone we love the tool to protect themselves. To be Italian American is to, in many ways, be part of a bigger organism than yourself. This way of becoming a village is present in many different places across the world; in many ways, there was no "becoming"—they were already a village and a single organism. People in the same town, in the same religion, or who have experienced similar things group together as a means of survival. We face difficulties in reconnecting and becoming one with the community in a capitalistic and white supremacist culture—one that tells us that to survive we are on our own. We have to pull ourselves up by our bootstraps, get into work, and monetize every aspect of ourselves in order to survive. Connecting with community allows us to not only recognize how our culture differs from that of our ancestors, but helps make space for us to navigate in what ways we have changed throughout generations or years.

Community is in many ways about mentorship, but it is also about creating relationships with the people around us who are fellow reconnectors of members of the culture. The chance to commune with and see the way other individuals practice, whether this is sitting in ceremony, participating in a workshop, or receiving knowledge from them which was shared with you, is an extraordinary opportunity. Learning from the layman and from the experience that other people have is in itself a way of reconnection, whether this is through watching someone you know cook a certain way or practice a particular ritual. The value of having individuals within your space that may not position themselves as teachers, but just as practitioners, and the ability to see the way they practice and share space, knowledge, and community, is a way of learning. In certain traditions, sharing information with peers and members of your community is an act of reconnection, but even within these cultures people may want to share knowledge in different ways. I am uncomfortable positioning myself as a teacher of Italian American folk magic; however I am very open to sharing certain practices contained within my folk magic with both my online community and my friends. I perform *mal'occhio* cures for others at work or in private and will make *breve* bags and other apotropaic charms when prompted. Several of my friends and peers in and outside of my community have been able to see me in ritual or performing elements of my folk magic throughout my reconnection journey. Although there are always elements of my practice and my culture that I refuse to share, especially the prayers I utilize within my cures and certain methods of transmission within the folk magic.

Historically and from an Italian American perspective, many ways of being would have been transmitted and passed down through family or even from neighbor to neighbor. You may have more well-known teachers, such as those documented as healers within the area who knew more than the average person, but many members of *Sud Italia*, or South Italy, were familiar with folk medicine or ways of folk healing. A daughter may have it passed down to her from a mother, the mother from the grandmother, or they may be passed down from aunt to niece or nephew and so on and so forth. Ways of cultural being weren't necessarily taught, they were intrinsic to living within a community of a certain culture. When we recognize that many things were not formally passed down, we can also recognize the importance of gathering in community, not positioning oneself above another, and learning from each other as individuals on the same journey together. Learning from a teacher is incredibly important in regard to initiatory practices or practices with roots in specific lineages, but sometimes our greatest teachers are not teachers at all. Rather, they are our peers who hold space for collective discussions, transmission of information, sharing of knowledge between different members of the culture—both reconnectors and those born within it.

Most of my learning about my practice, culture, and folk magic was imparted to me by members of my community who I created relationships with—even if they were over the internet. In an age where everything is digitized, community comes in many forms and it requires us to be more discerning, careful, and intentional with where we lay down our roots and who we form connections with. It's more difficult over the internet and social media to know someone's true intentions or ideas about you—and in many ways, community allows us to have access to information about individuals we may not know well, but others may. It allows us to receive second opinions about our feelings and intuition around content someone puts out. It provides us with a network of people who can tell us about their experiences with someone we may not know much about—which also requires our discernment. It requires us to formulate our own boundaries—both energetic and physical—and understand what we want in community, teachers, and mentors. It requires us to hold firm to those boundaries and understand that standing in our power, knowing our limits and what is and isn't okay for us in a teacher and peer, will be the most beneficial to our forming and gathering in community.

Our community expands beyond our physical and living peers and teachers and into our dead and spiritual teachers in the form of ancestors, herbal allies, our Mighty Dead or ancestors of our community, and identity (see more on page 81), and even spirits that were important to our families, such as saints, deities, plants, and more. Our ancestors, similar to what my teacher, Lisa, said, are part of us. All we have to do to connect with them is recognize them and reach inside of ourselves to learn from them. My mother often says to me, "When something is right, you will know" and I have found it to be true. With the guidance of my ancestors, I've been able to trace and receive rituals and develop relationships with plants that, upon discussing them with peers or family members later, are incredibly similar to live folk traditions or were important to my family. Our capacity for cultural reclamation allows us to connect with our ancestors, living and dead, who guide us and allow us access to information and practices that we may have lost or that may have never been transcribed—just passed by word of mouth. Ancestral reclamation does not, in any way, allow us access into closed practices or practices guarded by initiation. However, it can and will guide us to the right teachers, information, sources or rituals when we begin to truly embody our ancestors through veneration, reconstruction, connection, and healing ancestral trauma.

PUTTING IT INTO PRACTICE/ EVERYDAY CONNECTION

Connection happens to us every day. We interact with multiple people throughout our day as we go about our life while working, running errands, and even engaging on social media. As reconnectors, we can begin to mindfully and intuitively connect with those around us that are part of the culture we are working to reclaim and reconnect with, as well as utilize resources and research to further our understanding of cultural context, beliefs, superstitions, and practices.

This section of the book dedicates itself to exercises, resources, and actual ways to incorporate reconnection into your day-to-day life.

REACH OUT TO A COMMUNITY LEADER IN YOUR CULTURE
This exercise requires you to go a little bit outside of your comfort zone! Choose someone you regard as a community leader—this may be a teacher, peer, author, or academic—who

has contributed something you value within your reconnection journey. Ask them if they would be willing to sit in community with you and answer questions you have about their work or just to have an open conversation. Areas of conversation can include:

1. What inspired you to begin this work?

   ....
   ....
   ....
   ....
   ....
   ....

2. What did your journey look like to get here?

   ....
   ....
   ....
   ....
   ....
   ....

3. When you began to teach/write/research this work, what feelings did you have about the process?

   ....
   ....
   ....
   ....
   ....
   ....

4. What is your favorite part of being within this community and doing this work?

....
....
....
....
....
....

5. What aspect of the community do you feel is most reflected in your work?

....
....
....
....
....
....

PART 3

ANCESTORS, ANCESTRAL PRACTICES, AND PLANT ALLIES

One of the most important questions we can ask as we begin a journey of reconnection with ancestral practices is: "who are the ancestors?" Recognizing who our ancestors are—living, deceased, holy and not holy, helps us recognize those we are working to honor and connect with. Ancestors, contrary to popular belief, are not just ancestors of blood that have passed away, but ancestors of community, plant and animal ancestors, and adopted and fostered ancestors. In the book *Honoring your Ancestors*, Mallorie Vaudoise discusses a plethora of ancestors including, but not limited to, land spirits, ghosts, saints, blood ancestors, lineage ancestors, and more (Vaudoise, 2020). The ancestors we can venerate are an expansive group of individuals that we can honor and bring into our lives, regardless of religious belief and background, to help us reconnect. We know from genetics now that we carry our ancestors with us in our DNA. The experiences of our ancestors, including displacement, generational trauma, and memories are carried within us in ways we can only begin to imagine. Throughout our lives, we are changed by those around us, whether or not we are related to them by blood. Furthermore, each community you are working to reconnect to identifies its own ancestors differently. Every community has a unique and individual way of relating to its ancestors. Specific delineations of groups, subgroups, and categories will be different depending on cultural context. The lists in the following sections may be a great jumping-off point for your ancestor veneration, but you may find that not every subgroup contains every category.

HUMAN ANCESTORS

Our human ancestors include blood ancestors, lineage ancestors, and our Mighty Dead. While some of the ancestors in the "Spirit Ancestors" section (page 85) could be considered human, I chose to separate them based on how directly we are linked to the ancestors. Spirit ancestors are more of a spiritual connection while human ancestors represent those that are our direct family via community, adoption, blood, or identity.

LINEAGE ANCESTORS

Lineage ancestors represent human ancestors that are not a direct part of our bloodline, but still part of our family via adoption or partnership. An example of this is your partner's ancestors, such as parents or grandparents, or your parents or grandparents as an adopted individual.

BLOOD ANCESTORS

Blood ancestors represent human ancestors that are directly related to us via blood, your family members that you are related to.

THE MIGHTY DEAD OR ANCESTORS OF COMMUNITY

The Mighty Dead are ancestors who share identity, place, or traits with you. They are not directly linked to you by blood or marriage, but may be linked to us via how we identify or who we are. Examples of lineage ancestors include ancestors of sexual identity or creative identity. An example of the Mighty Dead are LGBT elders and teachers that we can venerate or deceased members of our work field.

NON-HUMAN ANCESTORS

Ancestral ties extend back beyond when we were living people—it allows us connection to plants, animals, and land that we carry with us as part of the ancestors.

ANCESTRAL PLANT ALLIES

Ancestral plant allies are those that our ancestors worked with, considered sacred, or even shared space with. These could be plants that grew in your ancestors' town, plants used in traditional cultural dishes, or plants used in medicine or magic within your ancestors' region. Certain ancestral plant allies that I work with include rose, which was important to my grandmother, and rue, which was important to my great-grandmother.

LAND SPIRITS

Land spirits can include the spirits of mountains, forests, and rivers of your ancestral lands. If you are from Sicily, you may feel a pull to venerate Mount Etna. If you are from Calabria, you may feel a pull to venerate La Sila, a mountainous evergreen forest located in the South of Italy.

ANIMAL ANCESTORS

Animal ancestors may be animals that were important to your ancestral lands, religion, or even your ancestors themselves. An example I have of an animal ancestor in my practice is the wolf. The wolf as an animal in Italy represents the birth of Rome, the Divine Mother, and furthers associations with several different ancient deities, such as Diana and Hekate (who have associations with dogs). Animal ancestors may also be those that are considered sacred or even common ancestors in your ancestral lands and region.

SPIRIT ANCESTORS

Spirit ancestors are ancestors that don't fall into our human ancestors or non-human ancestors categories. They exist through ties of place, religious and cultural history, or are not human.

SAINTS

Saints are my first example of spirit ancestors—while many consider these to be human ancestors due to the fact that many saints were humans who performed miracles, I consider the category of saints to be more in the spiritual realm. They are ancestors as well as spirits that are able to perform miracles due to the achievements in their life or after death. Contrary to popular belief, you do not have to be a Catholic to work with saints—they extend beyond Catholicism into many different traditions and religions, especially those that syncretized with Catholicism.

SPIRITS OF PLACE

Spirits of place are those that may be tied to your ancestral homeland or spirits that your ancestors acknowledged and worked with. Every tradition and culture has a different form of acknowledging spirits of place, such as crossroads, household, and landmark spirits. Spirits of place are tied to us in a similar way to saints—we are not directly related to them, but they held importance to our ancestors by tradition, culture, or religion.

PIECING TOGETHER WHAT YOU ALREADY HAVE

After we understand who our ancestors are, we can begin learning about them from what we already have access to. This begins in recognizing culture, no matter how watered down, in our existing lives and within our families. For some individuals reconnecting, there may be little to no recognition of your ancestors' culture in the present day—that's okay. However, for some reconnectors, the pull to reconnect may come from an understanding that something was lost or watered down and feeling the need to bring it forward into the spotlight again. There may also be a cultural identity tied to your ethnicity that you are already aware of and wanting to connect to. This section breaks down the process we can work with to collect what culture is left behind, tracing ancestry and family trees, and how to approach extended or direct family for information in different situations.

I grew up with some remnants and aspects of Italian American culture in my life. I didn't realize it until later, of course, since certain major aspects of the Italian American identity had been left behind—namely, Catholicism and existing in Italian American enclaves. Some elements of this diasporic culture that I grew up with included Christmastime trips to see my Italian American family (and a large emphasis on Christmas Eve dinner), food, and certain beliefs that were passed down to me that hold elements of beliefs about *mal'occhio*. I was raised to never say something I didn't mean—this didn't mean not giving compliments or not being kind, but rather that superficiality or falsehoods about someone meant less than a truly well-intentioned compliment. When I complimented someone or said they were pretty, my mother would tell me that pretty isn't everything—what is something about their personality that you like? In part, this was my mom trying to raise me and my sisters to prioritize how we were treated and how someone made us feel over their looks—but the push against prioritizing superficiality paid off for me as an older individual reconnecting with Italian American culture. When *mal'occhio* is transmitted, the envy or jealousy is unintentional and doesn't necessarily just include how someone, looks or what, they're wearing. It can also include someone's success, passion, partner, or accomplishments. I still feel as though the push from my mother to reconsider why I was complimenting someone, and for what, assisted me while growing up and in my reconnection journey—it's rare that I don't say what I mean or don't recognize my envy or jealousy of someone very quickly and how it may affect them.

I was also raised in a family where praise was limited—not that it did not exist or wasn't given, but teasing was the major form of love language and words like "I love you" were meant to be special and seldom used. When we look at beliefs in Italy about *mal'occhio*, compliments, and unintentional envy, it makes sense that it was worth more to tease and leave praise for when it was truly warranted. I was definitely raised in a home that was more comfortable giving compliments and praise than the house my mother was raised in, but there's still an element of my beliefs that struggles to accept compliments when they're given, primarily because I often feel as though they're ingenuine or superficial.

There's an element to diasporic culture that shows how this belief is changing—we know, as humans, that not receiving praise is harmful to us. A lack of compliments or praise from people we appreciate and look up to can lead to issues later in life, whereas too much praise may directly oppose our cultural beliefs about how *mal'occhio* and envy are transmitted. Diasporic individuals and reconnecting individuals from Italian American culture are being faced with the reality that our difficulties in receiving and giving compliments may be passed down through a mix of ancestral beliefs, but resorting to giving no compliments or praise to the people we care about tends to do more harm than good. It's possible for us to consider the cultural context and beliefs that caused this lack of compliments or discomfort around compliments in the first place, but also to begin to heal the idea that any compliment or praise may be the product of jealousy rather than a well-meaning statement. In many cases, these changing and shifting beliefs and the realization of problematic habits that have been passed down, generation to generation, are an example of the ways in which the folk continue to evolve and change over time. This expands into collecting what we already have access to by talking with those around us about particular beliefs that they grew up with, thus allowing us to recognize how they have filtered down into what we were raised with and taught.

Piecing together what you have also includes looking at the ways in which our families pass down traditions, what traditions are important, and how they honor their ancestors in their day-to-day. Rarely when we discuss reconnection do we discuss analyzing and looking at the remnants of ancestral veneration, tradition, and culture around us. Traditions such as Christmas Eve dinner, ideas around Befana, the Christmas witch, the importance of frugality, and the gifting of charms are elements of my family's beliefs that continue to persist in my practice and in my day-to-day life. There are also elements of Italian American culture that my family left behind—my mother left the Catholic Church as a child, and the idea of being part of an Italian American community including the sentiment of "family above all else" wasn't as present in my life growing up. Individuality was important, but I also grew up in a family where neurodiversity and chronic illness were present, and in many ways, we were forced to do things differently. My immediate family continues to be one of the strongest bonds I hold in my life—and I realized later that not everyone has this experience. I like to think that while I may not have grown up with an Italian American community or strong links to extended family that were Italian American, I grew up with a grandmother, grandfather, mother, father, and siblings who were there for me no matter what. When

my sister, father, and I were diagnosed with celiac disease, my grandma learned to make gluten-free biscotti. She bought a toaster that was dedicated for only gluten-free food to ensure that we could eat safely in her home when we visited. When I am in trouble, having a hard time, or need assistance, I know I could go to my family (who continue to be close by) and have them greet me with open arms and open their doors to me. This is in many ways a privilege and I continue to recognize that and be grateful for it every day.

There's also an understanding in writing this section that not everyone may have pieces that are left behind or people they can go to to learn more—and that's okay. It means you're on a slightly different journey than I am. You may also be in a situation where the people you would call on to learn more from are people who don't support you, or have harmed you, and approaching them would hurt you and your mental health. In this case, I would implore you to do what is best for your well-being. Seek out the answers in places that are open and accepting of who you are. In part, this is imperative to reconnection and building community—we don't need to continue to hold or perpetuate the generational trauma our parents, grandparents, aunts and uncles have reinforced. We can seek out understanding in spaces that respect us and hold space for who we are while also holding space for cultural context and recognition of the culture we are working to reconnect to.

Holding space for your own identity as a reconnector as well as the culture you are reconnecting to is a delicate and important balance. To reconnect, we are prioritizing community, research, and beliefs, but that doesn't necessarily mean that we need to put ourselves in positions that compromise our mental health or identity as individuals. While many cultures, especially those that were more rural, have been part of a family, community, or village as an element of their identity, we have the ability and privilege to choose our community in ways that our ancestors didn't. We are able to recognize the ways in which certain beliefs are harming us and some of us have the ability to remove ourselves from those environments in ways our ancestors, and possibly even other family members, may not have been able to. We have the ability to seek out queer, neurodiverse, and disabled communities online—something that our ancestors certainly didn't have access to.

Our reconnection journey is in part recognizing and reconnecting with culture, but also reconnecting to and recognizing ourselves. What do we need in a community? How can we surround ourselves with people who recognize who we are and value us? How can we uphold and continue to uphold culture in our day-to-day in ways that venerate our ancestors while also honoring ourselves and our well-being and identities?

WHAT IS ANCESTOR VENERATION?

As Mallorie Vaudoise writes, ancestral veneration can be defined as "any ritual or spiritual practice that reconnects you with the people who came before" (Vaudoise, 2020). Ancestral veneration is the practice of bringing human and non-human entities into your practice and life in ways that honor them, create reverence for them, and work with them in a variety of ways. The ancestors represent a large group of spirits, so working with and veneration of them can look different depending on the person working to reconnect with them. When we reconnect with the individuals who are living in our life, we are often able to piece together examples of how our family may venerate ancestors in the day-to-day. This could be through the passing on of recipes, festivals, ancestral altars, belief in guidance from them, storytelling, or even ideas of when or how to visit graves and cemeteries.

Ancestor veneration allows us to move beyond the veil and begin working with the dead, non-human spirits, and divinity in order to connect with culture and ancestry. Reconnection is in many ways a process of research and practicality as well as a spiritual process. When we work to reconnect to culture, we are also working to reconnect with our ancestry, ancestors, and reclaim the heritage they left for us. Ancestral veneration allows us access to information and confirmations that aren't always explainable. I once received information around a spell that I was meant to perform—it required a specific moon phase, red string, and four coffin nails. When I later talked with a peer who was raised in the tradition about how I received the spell including materials and how it was performed, they shared that there was an incredibly similar ritual that they had learned as a child growing up in the tradition to protect the home. This was one of many instances around how my ancestors communicated certain materials and ideas to me that I would later find out are present in living practices of other Italian Americans or practices present fifty to a hundred years ago in Italy with similar ingredients and premise.

Ancestral veneration is present in a multitude of cultures across the world in a variety of ways. Some of this includes holding space and creating an altar or memorial for ancestors who have passed on, ceremonies on the anniversary of an ancestor's death, creating a space to frame family photos and pictures which may have familial belongings, festivals, and more. A few common celebrations for ancestral veneration in the Western world include the Day of the Dead, widely observed in Mexico, All Saints' Day, a Christian holiday, or All Souls' Day in Italy. The celebrations of All Souls' Day in Italy can often include trips to cemeteries, flowers, prayer, and food, and depending on the region, rituals may differ slightly. In Sicily, children who are good and remembered their dead relatives throughout the year receive gifts sometimes hidden throughout the house. In the Emilia-Romagna region of Italy, the poor are entitled to receive *carita di murt* or charity in the name of the dead. Foods such as *fave dei morti* and *ossi dei morti*, which are both cookies, are customary foods (Phelan, 2022). Dee Norman, in her book *Burn a Black Candle*, shares her *ossi dei morti* recipe and discusses more about ancestral veneration and work as an element of Italian American folk practice (Norman, 2022). The ceremony of *jesa* found in Korea as well as other East Asian cultural spheres represents a ceremony to honor an ancestor, and ritual services or ancestral veneration in Korea have a long and rich history (Lee Kwang-kyu, 1984). Ancestral reverence and veneration permeate not just the lives of reconnectors, but varying cultures, religions, and spiritual practices.

Ancestral veneration is, in many ways, both a recognition of our ancestors as well as a focus on how to bring them, their culture, and their influence into our lives. Ancestor veneration, in many ways, is intrinsic to our very being. It is natural to honor those who have passed before us and to turn to them for guidance. It is natural to seek out saints, spirits, and guides to learn from them, especially those that may have helped those who came before us.

When we are understanding ancestral veneration and how to bring it into our lives, we can look at several different methods and ideas surrounding how to honor and bring them into our day-to-day practice.

VENERATION AND RITUAL

While all elements discussed here are ways of venerating your ancestors, this section focuses on more ritualistic methods of honoring them, including touching on the building of ancestral altars and altar-tending rituals. While the other sections described elements of veneration that take place outside the altar and within day-to-day, this section breaks down elements of ancestral veneration that may be more personal, such as offerings and communication. Our ancestral veneration can start in many different areas and in ways we may not expect, but for me, ancestral veneration and work began with an altar and paying respect.

An ancestor altar is a place of veneration for your ancestors, and it can look different depending on your culture and practice. Not all communities, however, have a practice of ancestral veneration that includes an ancestor altar. An integral aspect of reconnection includes acknowledging the boundaries of the tradition one is reconnecting with. This doesn't necessarily mean you cannot choose to create an altar anyway, while respecting that the tradition itself does not include the practice. Sometimes you can have multiple ancestor altars, depending on which ancestors the altar is for, and some ancestors may ask not to be placed on the altar. Altars may include pictures of deceased family members, candles, offerings, or items that belonged to ancestors. My ancestor altar includes a white candle with the maiden name and surnames of my family on it, a small figurine of a rabbit that belonged to my grandmother, a statuette of Saint Mary, pictures of deceased ancestors, protective plants and stones, a small bowl of water, and a dedicated mug for offerings. Some of my friends' ancestor altars include devotional oils, flowers, altar cloths, religious items, and particular drinks and foods their ancestors enjoyed. For more about creating your own ancestor altar, see page 105.

Veneration and ritual around the ancestors can be different for each practitioner, but here are some of the methods of honoring my ancestors that I utilize in my practice.

OFFERINGS

Offerings are gifts of food, water, drink, and more that can be placed on the altar for your ancestors. Devotional activities can also be considered offerings to your ancestors.

HOW DO I GIVE OFFERINGS?
The process of giving offerings can be as simple or as complex as you like. In my practice, I typically set the physical offering on my ancestor's altar, sometimes going so far as to verbally declare that the food, drink, or water is made for them. A more complex ritual could be praying over the offering, lighting a candle for them while the offering is on their altar, or giving the offerings on particular days or festivals.

WHEN DO I DISPOSE OF THE OFFERINGS?
Depending on your comfort level and accessibility, some offerings like water, oil, or alcohol can sit on the altar for as long as you want. Food can be set out after it is cooked and remain out until you are comfortable. For me, this includes leaving food out for the duration of the meal that I devoted to them to make sure that one of my pets doesn't get to it. Depending on your tradition, there may be beliefs around feeding yourself versus your ancestors and spirits first or how you dedicate the offerings to them. When disposing of offerings, food can be put in the trash to make sure the wildlife doesn't get it, or if it won't harm the environment and local animals, it can be buried or left outside. Drinks are similar when disposing of them, although I typically leave drinks on my ancestor's altar until they either evaporate, or completely disappear . . .

WHAT OFFERINGS ARE APPROPRIATE FOR MY ANCESTORS?

There are a few different categories of offerings that can be given to your ancestors and ancestral spirits:

1. *Food and drink:* Water is a well-known spiritual offering across traditions and cultures for spirits, as are particular liquors like brandy, rum, wine, and tequila. Certain ancestors may have particular drinks they enjoyed or liked during their life as well as favorite foods. For my ancestors, coffee and biscotti are a great offering, but depending on which ancestors I am working to connect with I may change my approach. Traditional food and drink from your ancestral lands or diasporic culture are always a great option for offerings, as are foods that would be used during particular rituals or holidays.

2. *Money:* Coins are an offering that can be used to pay off debts to spirits or pay for something you are taking. Money offerings can also be given to ancestors who assist you in prosperity or abundance. It is common in certain traditions to leave three coins of the same type for crossroad or cemetery spirits that you are asking for assistance with a working.

3. *Smoke:* Offerings of smoke include incense, cigarette or cigar smoke, or even unburnt cigars and cigarettes. Depending on the ancestor or spirit you work with, they may prefer to receive incense that would be familiar to them, such as cathedral incense or a scent they enjoyed, or unburnt cigars or cigarettes if they smoked. Certain spirits can be fed cigarette or cigar smoke if they are helping you with a particular working.

4. *Candles:* If you were part of a family that went to church, you may be familiar with lighting a candle at church for a specific person. This could accompany a prayer, like a novena, or be an offering by itself. These kinds of offerings can also be made to saints as part of a petition or as an offering after the petition is fulfilled. White candles are great offerings for ancestors and ancestral spirits. Candles can also be dedicated or consecrated for your ancestors to bring them into a particular working or time when they are lit. I tend to anoint white pillar candles to place on my working altar to light for my ancestors and when I need their guidance. These candles are anointed with a specific oil that contains a large amount of ancestral herbal allies as well as anointed at particular festivals or times. I tend to choose times when I feel my ancestors closer to me or more present, such as All Souls' Day, Candlemas, or other holidays that they would have considered important moments to gather with family.

5. *Oils and waters:* Certain oils or herbs can also be given to your ancestors as offerings, especially elixirs or oils including ancestral herbal allies that were important to them. Certain liquors may have been used not only for their taste but for their apotropaic benefits, as Mary-Grace Fahrun mentions in her book around Centerbe, a liqueur made from one hundred herbs. Certain waters, such as Florida Water, Saint John's Water, rue water, or other spiritual mixes may be important or valuable offerings to your ancestors along with devotional oils. For an exercise in creating a devotional oil, see page 114.

6. *Miscellaneous offerings:* Jewelry, perfume, or other items that may have been important to your ancestors are fantastic offerings for them and ancestral spirits. You can dedicate rings that you wear, earrings, apotropaic charms,

and even stones to your ancestors and ancestral spirits. Certain perfumes that your ancestors may have worn or scents that your ancestors liked can also be dedicated to them. For instance, I wear rose perfume and keep some on my altar since my grandmother wore it every day. When I wear my *cornicello* (Italian horn charm to protect against *mal'occhio*) or my *mano figa* earrings, I am wearing them in devotion to my ancestors.

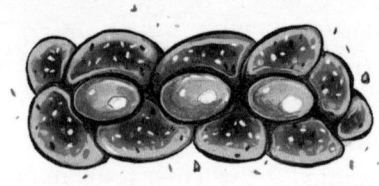

HOW DO I KNOW IF AN OFFERING IS ACCEPTED?

Different practitioners and traditions have different methods of deciding whether an offering has been accepted or not. The easy way to ask is by divining with tarot cards and seeing if you receive cards that are generally a "no" or generally a "yes" and acting accordingly. If you don't wish to divine, here are a few elements of my practice and personal gnosis that I have come to recognize as a "yes" or a "no" for offerings:

✣ An offering of drink or liquid evaporates: this is an accepted offering.

✣ An offering of drink or liquid evaporates quicker than expected or usual: this is an accepted offering, and an offering that these spirits enjoy and could be given more frequently.

✣ An offering of food hardens and stays looking the same, almost mummifying: this is an example of an accepted offering.

- An offering of food molds very quickly, such as a dry food in a dry climate molding overnight: this is a declined offering and one that probably shouldn't be given again.

- An offering of drink or liquid collects bugs or miscellaneous material: this is a declined offering. Be sure to rule out pest infestation, natural occurrences of moths, fruit flies, and other bugs before deciding that this is a spiritual occurrence.

- An offering of jewelry or physical item breaks or falls off the altar space: this is a declined offering. If there is a physical picture of an ancestor that spontaneously falls over, or knocks over images of other family members, this may indicate that this ancestor does not want to be placed next to other people and wants a separate space.

- An offering of a candle sputters out quickly after lighting: this is a declined offering.

- An offering of food molds in a natural or expected way, such as a piece of fruit molding after a week or so: the offering has been accepted and needs to be replaced.

- An offering disappears or is completely gone by the time you check on it (not eaten by pets or other animals): this offering was accepted.

ACTIVITIES

Activities refer to particular things that we do in our day-to-day life that our ancestors may have done or that work to bring our ancestors closer into our day-to-day life. This can include speaking the language, playing games, learning traditional methods of divination, cooking, and more. Activities represent areas of veneration that are things you can incorporate into your day-to-day life. For me, this includes divining with Italian playing cards that are used to play the game of Scopa and beginning to implement Italian dialect and language, including learning it. Activities may look  different for different reconnectors, and sometimes may include a variety of activities that fall into other categories. You may consider giving offerings to your ancestors or cooking specific meals part of devotional activities. You may consider meeting with community or learning more about cultural heritage part of devotional activities. In my practice, this area of veneration tends to consist of a few elements:

- Crafts and creations: this may be considered any creative activity that your ancestors once did, such as weaving, embroidery, sewing, cooking, writing, or brewing. In my practice, devotional activities that fall into this area include cooking traditional dishes, which I expand on later (page 107), creating *amari*, or Italian digestive bitters, and writing about certain topics.

- Language: this area often consists of learning language, speaking the language, or even doing particular research and activities that include my ancestors' language. Even consuming media in your ancestors' language is helpful to learn it. I consider praying in Italian, reading in Italian, and learning Italian part of this area. Some reconnectors feel a strong pull to learning and reclaiming endangered languages, particularly those that were outlawed, forbidden, or "lost" due to assimilation.

- Cultural immersion: this area is where you take part in activities that engage you in your ancestors' culture. This could be going to a festival, taking a pilgrimage (like those provided by Radici Siciliane), learning the language, watching a documentary or movie that was made in your ancestor's region, or listening to local music. Researching the culture of your ancestors allows you to more fully understand it. This area may also include visiting stores, enclaves, or allowing yourself to become part of the culture in a way you have restricted in the past. In this area, my practice includes communing with other members of my Italian American community, learning from them, and practicing the Italian language.

- Deconstruction: this is less talked about than the other areas of ancestral veneration, but is just as important. Deconstruction is, as reconnectors, looking critically at our role in white supremacy, our ancestors' traditions, and more in a way that allows us to see if they are and were problematic. Deconstruction requires us to be not only self-aware, but self-critical and critical of things that were passed down to us—including beliefs—that may be harming others or ourselves. When we are looking at things that came from the past, we will always come into contact with outdated or possibly problematic ideas and concepts that we need to reconstruct or possibly even dispose of completely.

- Traditional practices: this area applies to practices of folk magic as well as traditional games, rituals, festivals, and more. Traditional practices may overlap with activities in many ways—divining with Italian playing cards or playing

Scopa could be considered a traditional game or ritual, but it is also an activity. Traditional practices also line up with ideas around beliefs—*mal'occhio* healing in Italian American and Italian folk magic is informed by holding, or living, the belief of the existence of *mal'occhio*. This area of ancestor veneration also heavily depends on your culture and what practices, beliefs, and activities are present within. For my practice, this includes saints' festivals, divination with certain objects, and healing rituals. Rituals around birth and death, festivals and their corresponding beliefs and practices, and ideas around life markers are often great starting places to begin looking at traditional practices in your culture.

An important note

On page 211 we will talk more about problematic traditions and beliefs; however, within this section, it's important to mention recognizing our own contributions to white supremacy and racism as reconnectors. Oftentimes, our culture was lost through a need to assimilate or become "white." When our ancestors immigrated and left behind their culture in order to fit in, they were discriminated against and othered at first. Assimilating into whiteness and accepting white supremacy was the way to survive and sacrificing their culture was a way to ensure safety for future generations. In a way, every white person who grew up in a region like the US where racism is rampant was indoctrinated into racism and white supremacy from a young age, despite households of different ethnicities or ancestries still being different from typical White Anglo-Saxon Protestant, or "WASP", culture.

> *The system of white supremacy is insidious in several ways, including the need for individuals to leave behind culture, beliefs, or things that "other" them to "fit in." As someone who is racially white, it's important to note that learning to deconstruct white supremacy and becoming anti-racist is better learned from the voices who experience racism and continue to fight it every day. For resources on this topic, please see page 237.*

CREATING AN ANCESTRAL ALTAR

Creating an ancestral altar will look different for everyone, but this is the process I utilized to create mine.

1. Decide on a location where you would like your family to be present. Somewhere communal, such as the dining room, kitchen, or living room, is always a great option. Depending on your tradition, you may not want to place your ancestor altar in your bedroom.

2. Gather family photos or other mementos from your ancestors to place on the altar. These could be items that belonged to them or things that remind you of them. Fragrances that you associate with your family, jewelry that they owned are more ideas.

3. Choose items that you want to offer to your ancestors and incorporate into their altar—these could be a nice altar cloth, a candle, flowers, a glass of water, effigies of saints, or any other offerings you feel are appropriate.

After gathering your items, find a dedicated space, table, or even windowsill that has enough room for you to place your altar. If you want, you can cleanse the space with whatever materials you feel are appropriate in your journey. For me, this would be washing down the space with homemade rue water or cleansing it with a rue bundle.* If you want to, you can dress your candle with herbal allies or write down your family's names on the side of the candle (if it's a glass pillar candle). Spend some time deciding how you want to set up your items and family pictures. After you set up the items, you can do the following ritual to welcome your ancestors in.

Materials:

✢ White candle (prayer candle or pillar candle)

✢ Glass of water

✢ Anointing oil (optional)

---

* Please be mindful of handling rue if you are pregnant or breastfeeding.

Ritual:

1. Write out your family's names on a piece of paper or on the glass candle using a Sharpie.

2. Anoint the candle (if you want) with an olive oil or another oil that is important to you. Place your glass of water next to the candle. You can bless this water with whatever prayer you like, or verbally tell your ancestors that this is an offering by saying something like, "I offer this water to my ancestors so they are never thirsty in death." For blessing my water, I use nine Hail Marys.

3. After lighting the candle, say out loud your intentions for your ancestors. This could be along the lines of verbally declaring that your ancestors are welcome in your life and in your home. It could be asking them for their guidance and assistance in your life. An example of a verbal intention could be along the lines of, "Whenever I light this candle, I ask you to assist me in removing obstacles, and bring your guidance into my life."

To commune with your ancestors, you can create a devotional oil (see page 114), utilize traditional or non-traditional divinatory methods, or even spend time doing devotional activities dedicated to your ancestors (see page 101).

FOOD AND DRINK

Food and drink are an important element of reconnection. Cooking traditional foods and drinks, the sharing of meals and the passing down of recipes are ways that we continue to live on as our ancestors and venerate them in the modern day.

We are our living ancestors—we carry them inside of us, and when we eat things and feed ourselves food that they ate in the past or enjoyed, we are in many ways healing our connection with them as well as healing ourselves. In many cultures there are particular rituals, dishes, or drinks that are considered sacred as well as customs and rituals surrounding food, eating, and especially eating together. In Italian American and Italian folk magic, there are even beliefs surrounding particular ingredients or foods. If you spill salt, throw some over your left shoulder. It's unlucky to put bread upside down or set the table in certain ways. The fork and knife cannot cross as it will cause fights, and while you can have twelve dinner guests, thirteen is considered unlucky due to it being the number of individuals at the Last Supper. On New Year's Eve, particular dishes can be made to bring luck into the new year and certain types of foods are associated with abundance and prosperity in the home. Preparing particular foods, as Mary-Grace Fahrun writes, is magic.

For my Italian American family, food and communing at the dinner table or during special holidays was considered one

of the most important things we could do. My family would eat dinner together every night, even when we were angry or upset with each other or in bad moods. The only exception for this was when someone was ill, and when this happened food was brought up to them to make sure they ate. I grew up with particular dietary restrictions, so it was always better for me to eat at home since it mitigated the risk of cross-contamination. Due to a lot of traditional Italian and Italian American foods being inaccessible because of these dietary restrictions, it led to me having a relationship with food where I wholeheartedly understood that what I ate could either harm or heal my body. I later expanded on this in my spiritual practice and learned many ways to create traditional dishes in ways that were accessible to my body despite chronic illness, including following my intuition and ancestors' guidance around which foods were good when. I learned much of this from my mother as well, who has always been in the position of caretaker with two to three chronically ill individuals in the home. She is the one I go to when I feel sick or unwell due to my autoimmune disease, and she always recommends foods to stay away from or ones to consume to assist me in my healing. I also learned many different recipes and about ingredients that continue to be utilized in Italian American cuisine that were important to my family despite our restrictions. Recipes that were passed down were modified to better fit the needs of my family and certain foods were added in, but some things stayed the same, which I wanted to share here.

BROTH AND SOUP

Mary-Grace Fahrun discusses the importance of chicken or bone broth, or *brodo*, in her book *Italian Folk Magic*, writing: "*Brodo* is believed to have magical healing powers... Whatever the ailment, *brodo* is medicine. *Brodo* is also a valuable nutritional supplement when food is scarce. No matter how poor a family was, they could always afford bones to make *brodo*." Whenever we were sick, my mother would prioritize the use of bone broth. This could be a homemade chicken soup or a particular sauce or recipe where broth was added and many of our sauces and pasta dishes, especially tomato-based sauces, were slightly modified to include a little bit of broth. Bone broth, as it happens, is one of the best things to consume to promote gut health while also reducing inflammation. When we were sick because of our autoimmune illnesses, we knew to drink broth and probiotic-rich food. Of course, our ancestors may not have known this, but they did know about the magic of broth and the kind of healing that occurred when we consumed it. They didn't need an internet article or research paper to know this, they just needed to watch what happens when people who were sick or ill consumed broth over time to understand how important it was and how it helped aid recovery.

PASTA E FAGIOLI

Also referred to as "pasta fazool" in Italian American communities, *pasta e fagioli* was a staple dish in my home growing up. I grew up with the recipe containing meat, typically ground beef, broth, diced and strained tomatoes, gluten-free pasta and cannellini beans. My family typically used fusilli pasta to make *pasta e fagioli*, primarily because it's incredibly difficult to find ditalini pasta that's gluten-free. Every region and family may have a different recipe or use different ingredients—some may create a *pasta e fagioli* that's more of a chicken soup while others may change the quantity of tomatoes utilized in the dish itself. *Pasta e fagioli* in my family was not only one of my favorite dinners, but the dish that was cooked in the winter, on rainy days, or when we needed to be brought together. We would sprinkle a little Locatelli or pecorino romano on top and fought over the leftovers, which usually tasted better the next day. As I got older and began identifying as a folk practitioner and witch, I realized that not only was it a strong, hearty soup fantastic for warming the family up to each other but that the herbs utilized in the dish were those with correspondences to joy, love, luck, prosperity, and protection. Oregano is an herb that is well-known in love magic and for bringing joy into your situation, while basil is a fantastic herb for bringing in money and healing. Garlic, which was chopped up and warmed in olive oil with the meat until fragrant, is a vegetable that is known for its association to Saint Michael, even hung in braided strands inside homes to protect the inhabitants. While I know my family wasn't necessarily making *pasta e fagioli* consciously to heal rifts or bring in luck and love, it's undeniable that the ingredients and the dish itself are those that work a little bit of magic through healing—physically and emotionally.

SPAGHETTI AND CALAMARI

This dish is specific to Christmas Eve, and typically is only made on this night. In *Italian Folk Magic*, Mary-Grace Fahrun shares a spaghetti and clam recipe commonly made on Christmas Eve during the Italian American Feast of the Seven Fishes. This, in many ways, was my family's rendition of that feast which persists to this day. My mother would seek out calamari, strip and clean them and make a red sauce to include with them. This, similar to the meatballs my mother and grandmother made, is a recipe I don't yet have, but it is a dish worth noting due to how special it is.

MEATBALLS

Like every Italian American family, mine has a closely guarded and primarily secretive meatball recipe. To help you understand just how hard it is to get this recipe, I actually asked for it, and my mother's response was something along the lines of: "How do I know you won't give it to someone? I'm not giving you this." I learned very quickly that, like my grandma and my great-grandma, my mother tends to cook intuitively. While there is a specific formula for certain dishes, many times different ingredients are added depending on the needs of the people consuming the dish or what is readily available. Meatballs are a dish that you learn by doing and watching. You can't simply ask for the recipe and receive it, you have to earn it. This often entails being in the kitchen during the cooking and creation of the meatballs and actively contributing to the dish. Even expressing the desire to learn how to cook them and helping in the kitchen is in many ways a rite of passage and a step towards learning—although it takes quite a while to master them, especially when you have to make them gluten-free for a primarily celiac family. My mother's meatballs are different from my grandma's meatballs which were probably different from my great-grandmother's meatballs, but all of them have one thing in common—to learn to make them, you need to watch the process and be active in it.

TOMATO SAUCE

Different families and even different Italian American enclaves will call tomato sauce something different. Gravy, sauce, sugu, and ragu are all terms that may refer to a well-done sauce, and depending on your family, you may be familiar with sauce days or times when it is made in large batches to save for later. For my family, my mother would make a large pot of sauce and freeze it for future dishes or to eat with meatballs. Like *pasta e fagioli*, tomato sauce is made differently depending on family and the region your family came from. Ours typically includes strained tomatoes or tomato sauce, onions, and garlic. Tomato sauce could be added to a number of recipes, but was primarily used on spaghetti and in dishes where meat or meatballs were present. Another aspect of the sauce is that when adding ground beef, it became meat sauce which could be used with or without meatballs.

AMARO

A few years ago, I complained to my father of a stomach ache that wouldn't abate. I had tried water, resting, and several other methods with no relief. I was uncomfortable, annoyed, and didn't want to eat for fear that it would worsen. My father, who is not at all Italian, told me to wait and grabbed a bottle of Fernet-Branca, a style of *amaro*, pouring a shot for both me and my mother, who also had a stomach ache. He told me to drink it slowly to assist with my stomach, and within minutes, I felt infinitely better. When I asked him where he had learned this trick, he told me it was from my grandfather, and my mother added that her dad probably learned this from her grandpa. *Amari* are an incredibly important part of Italian and Italian American culture, often drunk as a digestif after meals. Different *amari* contain different herbs steeped in high-grain liquor that may have varying culinary, medicinal, or digestive purposes. Most *amari* recipes are kept under lock and key with only information around tasting notes or certain herbs

included, and different *amari* are used more regionally than others. Fernet-Branca was formulated in Milan, Averna was most likely created by Benedictine monks in the North of Italy, Cynar is a local liqueur from Termoli, and Braulio was made in Valtellina. Fernet-Branca found popularity in the US during prohibition, where it was labeled as medicine for cholera and still considered legal. You may have a liqueur or *amaro* that is frequently used by your family, even if they have no roots in its place of origin. For my family, Fernet-Branca, despite originating in a region incredibly far from my ancestors' Calabrian town, is the *amaro* of choice when it comes to healing stomach aches, due to its availability in the diaspora. I later began creating my own *amari* with different intentions and herbs to assist in different magical and mundane areas, and I still find that a small sip of the *amari* I make helps with stomach upsets.

COMMUNITY

While there is already a section on community as an integral aspect of your reconnection journey, this new section exists to emphasize the value of ancestral connection in the modern day. We are not our ancestors—we are new people with new beliefs, new environments, and new needs that our ancestors would not have experienced or imagined. To connect with community allows us not only to continue our ancestral veneration in the modern day and with modern individuals who are on the same journey as us, but also to discuss with others the ways in which our ancestors' beliefs and cultural practices may change or need reconstructing to make sense in today's world. For more about reconstruction of traditions, see page 221.

Community is in many ways an avenue for us to connect with living traditions, beliefs, and ancestors, as well as allowing us space to experience grief with people who understand.

CREATING A DEVOTIONAL OIL

Spiritual oils are found throughout different religions and traditions and are used for a variety of purposes. Oils and anointing oils have historical and even biblical uses in healing and ritual, especially those that are prayed over, prepared in certain ways, or made with certain herbs. In the modern day, it's incredibly easy to find a spiritual oil to assist you in a certain issue or with a particular spell. Just as much so, it's easy to create your own oil for an ancestor or ancestral spirit as a devotional activity to them.

Materials:

- A base or carrier oil; I prefer olive oil due to its importance in Italian folk magic.

- Dried herbs associated with the spirit or ancestor you are working to connect with and creating the oil for. In terms of saints, these may be herbs associated with them, such as garlic and angelica with Saint Michael, calendula, rose, and myrtle with Saint Mary, or herbs and scents that have similar correspondences to areas they rule over. Saint Peter could have a devotional oil including herbs associated with gates, roads, road openings, and uncrossings, such as chicory, camphor, and hyssop. For a particular ancestor, this could be their favorite flower, scent, or an herb they frequently used to cook with.

- ✛ Any objects or items that belonged to the ancestor or spirit you are working to connect with. This could be a charm or piece of jewelry that is passed down, a picture of them, or even dirt from their gravesite or the location of a *genius loci*, or local land spirit.
- ✛ A vessel
- ✛ High-grain alcohol
- ✛ Vitamin E oil (optional)
- ✛ Essential oil (optional)

Once you collect the herbs you associate with this ancestor or ancestral spirit as well as a chosen carrier oil, you can then begin to create your devotional oil. I prefer to light a candle in honor of the spirit or ancestor I am working to connect with through the oil before beginning this process and anointing myself with any ancestrally aligned oils.

Ritual:

1. Clean out your oil vessel with soap and water.
2. After letting your vessel dry, sanitize it with high-grain alcohol. This limits the amount of bacteria in the vessel and makes sure the oil and material do not mold.
3. While allowing your vessel to dry out, bring together your herbs and items that represent your ancestral spirit or ancestor.
4. With each herb, hold it in your hand and tell it why you are choosing it for this oil. Ask it to assist you in connecting with the ancestor or ancestral spirit the oil is for.

5. For your items that represent the ancestral spirit or ancestor, you can choose to either submerge them in the oil or place them around the oil to charge it with the energy of the spirit or ancestor. Charms that were passed down, pictures, or treasured items may not be things you want to submerge in the oil.

6. After your vessel dries, add in the herbs and items you are comfortable with submerging in the oil. If you want to state an intention for the oil, such as protection, spirit communication, or guidance, now would be the time to recite it over the ingredients.

7. Layer the base oil over the herbs slowly. As you are pouring the oil, feel free to verbally speak to your ancestors. You can dedicate the oil to them by saying something like, "I make this oil in your honor, and I ask for your assistance in communicating with me when I wear it." You could also write this intention, or any other requests for your ancestors.

8. If you want to, you can add essential oils for fragrance and vitamin E oil to help preserve the spiritual oil. For essential oil, ten drops per ounce is the recommended amount.

9. Shake your oil and then store it away from sunlight and heat.

10. The items that you chose to represent this spirit or ancestor, but that you don't want to submerge in step five, can now be placed around the stored oil to help charge it.

With most of the spiritual oils I make, I wait for a full moon cycle (thirty to thirty-one days) before using the oil, oftentimes making changes or adding more ingredients during that period or after the testing period. Feel free to decant your oil into smaller bottles and store accordingly, or keep in the original "mother oil" jar and use when needed.

A final note I would like to make in this chapter is that ancestral veneration and ancestral work are different. You can venerate your ancestors without working with them—especially if you find them to be problematic or difficult to be around. I truly only work with one or two branches of my family, but I venerate all of my ancestors, even those that need healing and that I don't get along with. To venerate is to regard with great respect, and is separate from worship, which is specifically about showing reverence and adoration for a deity. I was taught that we can venerate spirits, ancestors, and saints, but we cannot worship them—that worshipping is an act reserved for divinity. To "work with" is a term I often use in reference to ancestors and spirits—I am working with them to bring them into my life or they are very interwoven with my life in many ways. They may be assisting me in multiple different areas. When I am asking a spirit or saint for help with a specific problem, I refer to this as petitioning or a contract. It is very transactional, often asking for assistance with protection, abundance, or a specific issue with an offering as an exchange if they fulfill the petition. When I refer to my goddess, I will most likely say that I am devoted to her or a devotee of hers, which means that I have devoted myself and my life to worshipping and working with her and see her as my patron. I always encourage individuals to research differing opinions, especially on terminology surrounding folk practices and folk beliefs, but within this book, these are the terms I will use to explain the different ways I commune and interact with a variety of entities.

SAINTS, REGIONAL AND ANCESTRAL SPIRITS, AND DEITIES

Depending on which culture and tradition you are working to reconnect to, there may be active or syncretic beliefs or veneration of particular deities, folk or canonized saints that are petitioned frequently within your family or culture, or beliefs surrounding spirits that are regional to your ancestral lands which are present in the culture. Regional spirits can be categorized as beliefs around ghosts or hauntings, land spirits, crossroad spirits, or other spirits of location that are important within the culture. Saints can be both canonized by the Church, or folk saints that are present in cultures heavily influenced by folk Catholicism. Deities could be part of a living or ancient religion that existed or continues to exist. In Italy, ideas and rituals surrounding particular Greek and Roman goddesses were adapted into rituals or ceremonies surrounding particular saints and apparitions of Mary. Several important holidays surrounding goddesses, such as the feast of Nemoralia for *Diana Nemorensis*, were overshadowed by the Assumption of Mary, set two days after the original holiday. The original festival of Nemoralia included lighting torches to carry around Lake Nemi, women and children adorning their hair with flowers, and prayers tied to trees with prayer ribbons.

Imagery that was largely associated with pre-Christian divinity filtered down into saint veneration and worship, writes Sicilian American cultural historian Lucia Chiavola Birnbaum in *Black Madonnas*, "In spite of church interpretation of Lucia as a pious virgin, popular customs tap into submerged beliefs that remember her as the pagan Sabine mother goddess, Juno Lucina, 'mother of light'" (Birnbaum, 2000). Saint Lucy or Santa Lucia is regarded as the saint of light, protecting against the evil eye and celebrated on 13 December with bonfires and torches to expel the winter darkness. Whole-grain wheat or couscous is a traditional ingredient used to celebrate Santa Lucia and represent her eyes, which were cut out but then miraculously restored in death. Lucia, in her iconography, is usually shown holding her eyes on a plate in front of her—these organs, especially, hold influence and importance in the controversial work of Marija Gimbutas, alongside other imagery found in Paleolithic and Neolithic artifacts (Birnbaum, 2000). Certain temples and shrines to particular black Madonnas were built on the remains of older goddesses' temples, as was the case of the black Madonna of Santa Maria in Ara Coeli, which was built on the site of the Temple of Cybele, the church of the whitened black Madonna in Cosmedin, which was built on a temple to the goddess Ceres, while the temple of the Madonna of the Mountain at Polsi originally contained two shrines—one to Aphrodite and one to Persephone—that were later syncretized. While goddess worship and veneration are not conscious or active in Italy, veneration of the Madonna, especially the black Madonna, patron saints, ideas and beliefs about regional spirits stemming from earlier animistic practices, and syncretism from earlier religious beliefs are present and alive in both Italian and Italian American culture.

REGIONAL SPIRITS

Regional spirits refer to local rivers, lakes, mountains, forests, and other natural phenomena as well as spirits that may travel distances, such as the elements (wind, water, earth, and fire) and any spirits of specific location that are mentioned in your ancestors' practice or culture. This could, in part, be an animistic practice within your culture or even recognition of particular landmarks and important areas (cemeteries, crossroads, railroads) as places where spirits dwell and can be petitioned for particular things. Regional spirits may also include patron saints of your local area or your ancestors' hometown. For more on saints, see page 126. Regional spirits and approaching regional spirits will be different for every practitioner, family, and culture. While Italian folk magic is heavily syncretic with Catholicism, I find that animism and animistic practices, such as honoring local mountains, crossroad spirits, and forests, feel correct and fitting with my belief system and practice. Many cultures may have had animistic beliefs or honored and venerated regional spirits. This could include taking pilgrimages to landmarks to give offerings and ask favors or communing with different spirits of location for particular reasons. In ancient Roman animism, ideas of house spirits, crossroad spirits, vengeful spirits, and ancestors likely trickled down to influence aspects of our modern-day folk magic. An example of this was the celebration of Lemuria or

Lemuralia, a festival observed as an annual religious event that performed rites to exorcise malevolent and fearful ghosts, or lemures. In Ovid's detailed account of the festival, the symbol performed by the head of household to ward off ghosts—the taking of his thumb between his fingers—may have been one of the ancient examples of the *mano figa*, or the symbol to ward off the evil eye. Due to Lemuria, any time in the month of May was considered unfavorable for marriages —a belief that is still upheld due to the month being now dedicated to the Virgin Mary. To understand and learn more about regional spirits, there are a few steps you can take.

1. Learn about mountains and other natural phenomena that exist in your ancestral lands. This may be a nearby sea or ocean, a forest, or even rivers.

2. Look into superstitions and beliefs about how to interact with the natural world or specific locations, such as cemeteries, crossroads, and churches. Oftentimes superstitions and beliefs about these areas can tell us more about how our ancestors interacted with them. For instance, certain beliefs about crossroads and why we go to them can tell us more about how our ancestors perceived the spirits who reside there.

3. Look into ideas around the home and the upkeep of the home.

4. Look into local and regional features, such as mountains, forests, rivers, or spirits that exist near you.

5. Reach out to individuals within your culture and ask about landmarks that were important to them or those that still are.

6. If all else fails, move back a bit—look at the civilizations that came before you in this area and their ideas on spirits, landmarks, and how they were approached. From there, you can look for threads in the living culture and beliefs of the folk.

CONNECTING WITH REGIONAL SPIRITS ON STOLEN LAND

If you exist in an area that was colonized or away from your ancestral homelands, you may be confused on the appropriate ways to approach regional spirits. However, you can still venerate ancestral regional spirits in a different place. Meanwhile, it's important to recognize that the land you live on may have been stolen or colonized and the original stewards of it were forced out. We can learn about regional spirits that exist in our current region through prioritizing the voices of the Indigenous peoples. These spirits can be honored through recognition and through learning about them from Indigenous peoples and Indigenous written sources. Regional spirits may also overlap with beliefs and practices in your culture without you having to work with a spirit that belongs to an Indigenous culture. In some cases, a certain plant may be solely used in this culture, and taking classes with and learning from Indigenous teachers through classes, festivals, or writings can assist you in more fully understanding the plant. In some cases, as I've found, a plant utilized within your ancestral culture may also be recognized within an Indigenous tribe—my tattoo artist and I bonded over the mullein plant and its usage within both of our respective cultures.

Mullein, while considered invasive in some areas on Turtle Island, is still utilized for its medicinal properties by the

Zuni, Nahuatl, and other tribes for tea, powdered root to treat rashes, varicose veins, as well as ceremonial purposes. Mullein is also utilized and recognized in Italian American folk magic (as well as many other regional practices) as medicine for grief and respiratory support. Many of our ancestral herbal allies may be invasive, creating a difficulty in accessing them and cultivating them without harm to the local environment. Tending to your local spirits may include removing invasive species that are ancestral to you and creating a space where the *genius loci* and local wildlife can thrive. Holding space for the autonomy of plant spirits is also recognizing that a spirit in your local area or that you may not be familiar with in your ancestral lineage may ask to work with you and recognizing the difference between the commodification of the spirit versus honoring and veneration of the spirit. It's incredibly important to be mindful of plants that are already endangered, over-commodified, or difficult to access which are also sacred to Indigenous cultures, as choosing to work with them or bringing them into your practice without permission or learning the proper due course through a teacher or person of that culture constitutes appropriation.

This, however, is different from finding out about the wildlife of your yard, local park, or bioregion, and recognizing how best to learn about it, work with it, and create relationships with it. When I lived in Pennsylvania, my mother spent over a decade cultivating our yard to be a certified wildlife habitat. Many of the plants were native, and only some of them were those that held significance to my ancestors. However, I still formed relationships with them primarily through connecting with them, creating a bond, and utilizing them in my practice. As I began my folk practice and connecting with my ancestors, I realized that while cultivating a relationship with my ancestral plant allies was important, folk magic is defined by accessibility and what is available to you. In the case of my home in Pennsylvania, this was hydrangea, pine, dogwood, echinacea, and fern. My first *l'acqua di San Giovanni*, or water of Saint John, an Italian and Italian American folk ritual where one collects local flowers and plants to create a cleansing water, contained almost none of my ancestral plants because I had no access to them. Rather it was filled with flowers, leaves, and sticks from plants I had cultivated a relationship with over a decade in my yard. Overlap that exists with regional spirits could also include the honoring, veneration, and importance of local woodlands, mountain ranges, and rivers.

Working with, honoring, and venerating local spirits requires us to deconstruct the idea that something is automatically for us based on ancestry or locality—we need to listen and respond, and build relationships over time. Recognizing the spirits that call to you, continue to appear for you and seem persistent in their wish to help you—whether ancestral or local—allows you to begin to become familiar with their presence and recognize the best way to cultivate a relationship with them. This could mean an unexpected spirit, as in my case hydrangea, coming forward as an ally. This could also mean an ancestral spirit tells you no. Even when we receive a "no" for working with or venerating a spirit, that no tells us more about our journey, where we are going, and which allies may be ready to help us along the way.

Once you've identified regional spirits specific to your culture and local area, here are a few ways you can begin to connect with them:

✣ Leave environment-friendly offerings at the place where the spirit resides—this could be flowers that are non-invasive or not threatening to the bioregion, water, and anything biodegradable that won't harm the local wildlife.

✣ Familiarize yourself with the spirit itself—spend time learning what offerings they like, how they like to be honored, and stories about them.

✣ Learn how your ancestors worked with this spirit in their practice—did they have myths that originated around the spirit, like Mount Etna? Did they forage and find food there at certain times of the year, like La Sila? Did objects or items from the spirit's site hold value in their customs and beliefs, such as water from wells?

✣ Tend to the area around the spirit—if this is a tree, mountain, or creek that exists close to you, spend some time taking care of its surroundings. This could be picking up trash, weeding (if you are allowed), or overall keeping the area in good condition for other wildlife and spirits.

SAINTS

Depending on the culture and the tradition you are working to reconnect to, saints may play a role in the belief set or folk magic of your ancestors. Many saints are syncretized with earlier divinities in different regions or religions, such is the case with saints like Saint Peter in various African diasporic religions and Saint Mary and different epithets of Juno. The syncretism of saints (whether they are folk saints or canonized) isn't a chance for you to take them out of their cultural context—rather, a chance for you to recognize that there are many ways to approach them in varying cultures, practices, and belief sets. Saints are a part of many various religions, including but not limited to Catholicism, and are often petitioned or prayed to in traditions and cultures where the beliefs and culture have become syncretic with or heavily influenced by the Church.

Folk Catholicism is in many ways different from the Church and Catholicism. If you ever had a *nonna* that would drip oil into water to test for the evil eye, rub an egg on you when you were sick, you know that if you asked them what they were doing they would shrug, brush it off, or just refer to it as a thing they did. They may divulge more information about why they were doing it or they may not—and many insisted they were good Catholics who went to church every Sunday. The praying to and petitioning saints for a particular reason is an element of the Catholic religion and Church that is canonical, but who was prayed to, why it was done, and ideas surrounding which saint is the best to go to often give us insights into how saints play into our ancestors' culture and practices. Your family may even have a patron saint, or a saint that was gone to for difficult or impossible situations and was always regarded in a strong light. You may also have a patron saint that ruled over your ancestors' town or a saint that rules over your current area. Ideas around saints, who they are, and how they play a role in our practice, vary depending on the practitioner and the culture; however I will share my stance as well as a few other practitioners' stances to help you understand how a few folk practitioners approach things like saint work.

In my practice, saints represent people who have lived and died and who did miraculous things while they were alive or dead. They rule over particular areas, illnesses, and issues based on stories of them while they were alive, and they can be petitioned by people—whether you identify as a Catholic or not—to assist in a vast manner of situations. In *Black Madonnas*, Birnbaum writes, "Di Nola holds that in peasant religion there is a closer relation to local patron saints than there is to Jesus or to God. In popular beliefs, the Madonna becomes many local Madonnas regarded as sisters, whose function is protective" (Birnbaum, 2000). Ideas around patron saints being more powerful than Jesus continue to persist in different anthropological journals, such as *Italian American Folklore*, where Frances Malpezzi and William Clements write, "When the peasant leaves his native village, he will forget everything but his patron saint … The trouble is that he makes all kinds of bargains with him, ranging from offering to burn a candle before the image of the saint if the latter will help him to carry out a business transaction, to promising to bring a twenty dollar bill when the statue of the saint is to be carried through the streets if he can have the honor of being one of the bearers. A good lady said in reply to my question as to whether she had gone to church at Easter, 'I go to church on St. Anthony's day. He is my favorite saint and is more powerful than Christ, for he has performed more miracles than he. Besides, he is so handsome'" (Malpezzi and Clements, 1992).

These ideas around saints are often reflected in the way other Italian American practitioners discuss saint work. Mary-Grace Fahrun in her book starts the saint section with the following: "I first want to get one thing out of the way. You do not have to be Catholic or Christian to work with saints. Nor are all saints Catholic or Christian". Fahrun goes on to say, "Saints are magicians who once lived and, during their life here on earth, consistently performed great manifestations or spells that could not be explained away as coincidences" (Fahrun, 2018). Dee Norman, in her book *Burn a Black Candle*, echoes this sentiment, writing: "Someone who isn't a devout Catholic (me, for instance) understands that a saint is an entity with distinct areas of expertise or interest. In my eyes, whether a saint started out as a physical living being or not, they represent a force that humans can work with" (Norman, 2022). In my family, when we needed a miracle or something to truly happen, we didn't pray to God or Jesus—we prayed to a specific apparition of Mary. I grew up hearing about the power of my nana's novena to Our Lady of the Miraculous Medal. The prayers my grandma kept with her on paper that we found after she passed were not the Our Father prayers or prayers concentrating on Jesus, but a prayer to Saint Anthony of Padua, the rosary prayer, and the novena to Our Lady of the Miraculous Medal.

When I began my journey in reconnection, I didn't necessarily feel comfortable with approaching the saints, primarily because I still linked my connection with them to the institution of the Church. What ultimately helped me was realizing that I didn't have to identify as a Catholic or go to church to talk to the saints—I just had to approach them and ask for help. A lot of practitioners have varying approaches to working with the saints, and many still believe that you have to be

Catholic or concentrate on Jesus to implement folk Catholicism in your practice. The approach I use isn't necessarily one that everyone loves, but it is one that has gotten me results and allowed me to reconnect with prayers, practices, and beliefs that my ancestors held surrounding the power of saintly entities.

Needless to say, not every culture is syncretic with folk Catholicism and not everyone may have an interest in approaching the saints. While saints are beloved by many, certain saints can also be representative of the underbelly of bigotry of the times they lived in. Untangling, understanding, and holding space for the complicated history of saints is vital, especially in recognizing the way in which saints are vehicles for the harm of the Christian Church to marginalized populations. Here are more things to know about saints and about approaching them.

CATEGORIES OF SAINTS

Saints are not just those that are canonized by the Church—there are several types of saints that we can petition.

Folk saints

Folk saints are those that have not been canonized by the Church, but are still recognized by people as saints. Some of these saints are incredibly regional and cultural, including Santa Muerte, Saint Sarah, and Saint Guinefort the greyhound saint. Folk saints often receive local veneration from the folk or the people in the area for a variety of reasons. Some folk saints are well-known and their veneration has begun to travel—such as Marie Laveau—while others may be specific to people in particular ethnic groups, such as Saint Sarah, the patron of Romani. A few folk saints were later canonized by the

Catholic Church, while others represent both deities and folk saints, such as Maximon. Santa Muerte is a legendary folk saint seen as a personification of Death.

Canonized saints

Canonized saints are those that have been officially canonized by the Church, such as Saint Joan of Arc, Saint Lucy, and the Apostles. There can be overlap between folk saints and canonized saints, but this goes to show that the veneration of saints isn't just apparent in the Church—it belongs to the people and who they choose to uplift and venerate.

After we understand saints and who they are, we can look in more depth at how saints operate in your ancestors' culture and belief sets through a few methods.

Recognizing patron saints or saints that are important to your family

You don't have to talk to the saints that your family did, rather it's helpful to recognize the ways in which saints appeared and played a role in your ancestors' life.

- Research any patron saints that existed in your ancestors' hometown if you know it or saints that exist in your immediate area. The best way to do this is to look into local churches or Catholic parishes as well as any local shrines.
- Ask your family about the prayers your family recited and said or who they would pray to in particular situations.
- Take note of any home altars, statues, or candles that happen to be in your family's home (if you have access to it).
- Ask your family if anything in particular was done for certain situations, like selling a house, marriages, births, or deaths.

Exploring which saints you identify with

Your personal patron saint may be different from the saints your ancestors prayed to or felt connected to. You can explore which saints feel right for you by:

- Looking into the saints you are named after, if any. It's common for certain cultures to name their children after particular saints to put them under that saint's patronage.
- Looking into the saints who hold patronage over your identity or job.
- Looking into saints petitioned for a particular situation you need help with.
- Looking into saints that are commonly petitioned or venerated within your ancestors, and your culture.

Petitioning the saints

While researching saints is important and takes time, I found my family's and my patron saints through actually asking saints for assistance and seeing who gave me a response. Saint petitioning will be different depending on the folk and the culture, but below are a few ways I do it.

Burning a candle:
Lighting a candle with the image of the saint on it, or even a plain-colored candle in their honor, is a potent way to petition. Different saints have different colored candles, with a few listed here:

- Saint Expedite: red candles
- Saint Anthony of Padua: brown or white candles

- ☦ Saint Francis of Assisi: brown candles
- ☦ Saint Mary: blue or white candles
- ☦ Saint Michael the Archangel: red or blue candles
- ☦ Saint Peter: red candles

Different candle colors also have different meanings in the Catholic Church and are based on cultural beliefs, so choose what feels right depending on your understanding and beliefs surrounding the saints. For every day the candle burns, pray one day of a novena prayer to ask the saint for assistance with your petition.

Pray a novena to them:
Novenas mean different things in different cultures, but in my family, a novena always represented a nine-day prayer by itself. Novenas exist for all different saints and require you to pray to them every day for a full nine days. Similar to burning a candle as a petition, you can offer the saint something in return for fulfilling your petition included in your novena.

Write out your petition:
Writing out your petition allows you to place it physically under a figure of the saint or a candle burned in their honor, or you can anoint it with an oil dedicated to them. Written petitions are beneficial when you are calling on a saint for longer-term workings and assistance as the note can be placed in an oil or kept indefinitely.

A pilgrimage to their site:
While a pilgrimage can also be an offering, it's also a suitable petition. Shrines and churches typically have candles that

you can light for someone or as a request, and I like to do this whenever I travel to petition a saint.

I usually recommend that you offer the saint something in return for fulfilling your petition, such as public thanks, an offering they may enjoy, taking a pilgrimage to a local shrine or church of theirs, giving offerings to a church named after them, or even setting up a home altar for them. Below are a few offerings I've given to saints in the past:

- ✚ Saint Expedite: pound cake, an oil dedicated to him, a candle dedicated to him, alkanet powder.
- ✚ Saint Anthony of Padua: *amari*, a statue of him in the home, a glass of water, wine, bread, salt, fresh flowers.
- ✚ Saint Francis of Assisi: a brown candle dedicated to him, a prayer to him, medals of his.
- ✚ Saint Mary: a statue, an oil devoted to her, a rosary prayed to her, a physical rosary dedicated to her, candles, offerings of roses placed on her altar.
- ✚ Saint Michael the Archangel: a physical statue of him, a post about him, an oil devoted to him.
- ✚ Saint Peter: a prayer to him, a set of keys blessed in his name, talking about him to people.

DEITIES

Oftentimes, particular cultures have a dominant religion or set of beliefs that includes divine beings or deities. Some religions are monotheistic (Judaism and Christianity), polytheistic

(Shinto), henotheistic (Hinduism), or something entirely different. Theism, by itself, constitutes a belief in the existence of gods or a god. You can believe in many gods (polytheism), one god (monotheism), or even no gods (atheism). Just because a religion is dominant in your culture does not mean you have to identify with it or be part of it, but looking into how the religion informs the culture assists us on our reconnection journey. Divine beings that you are interested in researching or pursuing may not always be a recent part of the culture, beliefs, or practices of your ancestors—and that's okay. If they are, you may also have a relationship with them outside of the dominant religion. Or, alternatively, you may not be interested in working with the deities from your culture at all. "Deity worship" and "working with a deity" aren't required in order to reconnect with your ancestors; however it has been a part of my journey. As mentioned before, Dr Angela Puca, who studies Italian folk medicine and culture, describes a shift in modern-day Italian folk practices, wherein the newer generation is more likely to call upon pre-Christian deities rather than saints. Or, they combine the two. In my own experience, my recent ancestors remained vehement Catholics, which impacts my personal practice.

Worship and devotion to pre-Christian deities has not been dominant in Italian culture since ancient times; however the syncretism between saints and older practices is present wherever we look. Both Dee Norman and Mary-Grace Fahrun examine working with deities, especially Roman and Greek deities, in their books discussing their folk magic practices despite the practice not being predominantly documented or practiced in Italian folk magic. My point of view has always been that if we go back far enough, we would see that our ancestors did worship and venerate these gods, even if our most recent ancestors did not. We can look at syncretism as evidence for how ingrained certain beliefs and rituals became and how they transformed over time—but not as an excuse to ignore cultural context as we reconnect, which can oftentimes include religious context. Folk practices are holistic religious and spiritual systems—as we reconnect, we should take note of the holistic systems as much as we take note of the deities. As someone who identified as a witch and a pagan before identifying as a folk practitioner, I was incredibly comfortable incorporating the religion of my ancient ancestors by including pre-Christian deities into my practice. This choice, including the choice to venerate saints, will not be the case for every practitioner. Furthermore, not every individual comes from a culture in which polytheism is a thing of the past.

In many countries, polytheistic religions are the dominant religion, or at least a religion that is closely tied to the culture. In certain religions, you have to be initiated or a part of the religion to approach the spirits and/or divinity of the religion.

Even if the religion is "open," to remove the deity from the religion it originates from is to ignore myths, beliefs, and how the divine being continues to function in the day-to-day life of the members of the religion. Deities and divine beings rarely, if ever, exist outside a religious construct or context. The religious context provides the ethos in which a spirit is defined. Again, we must learn about the ethos as much as we learn about the spirit. This isn't to say that deities or divine beings can't have reclamations or different uses and relationships with people outside the religion, like the Christian God, but to understand the source text and where the deity originates from is of the upmost importance. For example, I wouldn't begin working with Shakti without understanding the role that Shakti takes in the active religions she is a part of or without actually learning about Hinduism, its denominations, or without talking to or learning from practicing Hindus. Hinduism is, in many ways, a broad term and a religion including many different ways of life, sects, ethics, and more, and while some consider it an "open religion," it still requires cultural context surrounding the divine beings within the religion as well as the proper and respectful approach. As a living religion that continues to be practiced by thousands of people alive today, learning the context of the religion, how divine beings are traditionally worshipped, festivals, and more is of upmost importance. Even with religions that are no longer practiced, it's important to recognize the cultural and historical context from which the deity comes from. Think of it like this—if you do not understand the religion in which an entity was identified or worshipped, how well can you actually understand that entity?

Deities can be worked with for a variety of reasons in your reconnection journey, or even in general. Deity work and worship are historical phenomena, going back several centuries and found in a variety of religions and civilizations since the beginning of time. Depending on your tradition, culture, and which deities you are interested in, you can work with and worship them for a variety of reasons. In Homer's *Iliad*, ancient Hellenic deities influenced everything surrounding the Trojan War and various offerings—no matter how gruesome—were given to the deities to win their favor. One of the more famous offerings is the sacrifice of Iphigenia, Agamemnon's young daughter, after he shot and killed a sacred deer. Artemis influenced their movement by halting the wind and stranding the Greek fleet. Many of the Olympic gods took part in the war and influenced the outcome, allowing us to understand the ways in which ancient Greece viewed divine intervention as well as our own fates—a prophecy foretold that Achilles would die at Troy, and die he did.

Divine beings and gods can be approached through several different lenses. Some see the deities of their tradition as manifestations of archetypes, such as the Maiden, Mother, and Crone of Wicca. Ancient Rome, before its Hellenization and Etruscan influence, saw its deities as divine powers that did not have a physical form. Later, they were anthropomorphized and many syncretized. In Taiwan, ancestral shrines and temples are everywhere, and Taiwanese individuals may identify as Buddhist, Taoist, or Confucian while also implementing elements of folk beliefs and practices to fit their needs (Quartly, 2016). Religions subscribing to pantheism, such as Taoism and Hinduism, believe that divinity and the universe are the same, rather than separate things. Pantheistic religions eschew ideas of transcendence, or of divinity being beyond reality, asserting that divinity is present in the universe and therefore is reality. By contrast, most Christian denominations believe that God created the world and transcends reality. Polytheism, sometimes seen in contrast to pantheism, is the worship of and belief in more than one god, while omnism is the respect of belief in all religions with their gods or lack thereof. Deities and divinities can exist as ruling over certain things, such as the harvest, and be petitioned for assistance in these areas. Depending on your reconnection journey, you may find that certain approaches to divinity will come more naturally than ideas you were raised with. Or, the beliefs you were raised with differ from the cultural perspective with which you are reconnecting.

I was raised by an ex-Catholic mother who, in hindsight, seems to have a relatively pantheistic and animistic point of view. I find that in my devotion practice to Diana, I tend to see her as ruling over certain things or separate from aspects of the world while also being present in nature and elements of such. I tend to feel as though the spirits of animals and trees are related to, but separate from, Diana herself. Similarly, the mountains and crossroads I visit to commune with Diana are related to, but separate from, Diana. Regardless, in these experiences I felt as if Diana made herself present, just as those in ancient Greece and Rome connected to Diana through nature. I view Diana's divinity as separate from the divine conceptualizations of the Christian God. For example, I don't feel as though she is the creator of the universe, but rather a being who resides in and watches over certain parts of the universe.

Deity work doesn't need to be complex in order to make a difference in your practice, nor do you need to know your beliefs around the universe and divinity before beginning to research and explore devotion or worship of a deity. Cultural understandings of divinity and what divinity means will change depending on what culture you are reconnecting with. Here are some of the ways I began researching and connecting with Diana:

1. Look at regional divinities—are there temples or shrines that existed close to your ancestors' homeland or that still exist in this area?

2. Look at cultural religions and deities—what is practiced in your ancestors' homeland? Is there an earlier or local religion that was syncretized with Christianity?

3. What divinities hold cultural importance in your ancestors' homeland?

4. Were there ancient religions and cultures that were present in your ancestors' homeland, if any?

5. How does the current culture of your homeland and that of your ancestors reflect the living or ancient religion?

6. Does your family have a particular patron deity or a deity they go to when things need to get done?

7. In your ancestral homeland are there any regional legends, myths, or stories that relate to a particular divinity or set of divinities?

If you're not able to answer these questions, or if you believe your ancestors only worshipped the Christian God, I would encourage you to expand your understanding of syncretization. Many pre-Christian spirits in Europe were preserved through folk belief, folk practices, and folklore. Even if there is not a particular deity you can link to your ancestors (outside of the Christian God), was there a particular figure from folklore important to your ancestors? What about your ancient ancestors? You may be pleasantly surprised to learn how many pre-Christian spirits lived on in superstitions and folk tales. When you realize what deity you feel connected to or want to worship or devote yourself to, you can begin actually researching and implementing elements of working with the divinity in your daily life. To begin connecting with a deity, you can:

✢ Look into primary sources surrounding the mythology or legends of the deity.

✢ Begin researching worship or ancient cults or sects that worshipped the deity.

✢ Research past or live cultural context surrounding the deity you are interested in working with.

- Look at herbal associations, epithets, and traditional offerings for the deity.

- Connect with an initiate if the deity is from a closed religion or practice and receive advice on beginning your initiation journey.

- Visit a shrine, temple, or worship site of the deity to familiarize yourself with typical offerings and imagery.

- Look at how the deity functions within a living or ancient religion—are/were there specific holidays on which they were celebrated? What rituals or offerings were given as part of their worship? What role did they play in the religion?

As you begin this process, remember that lasting, healthy relationships often take weeks, months, or years to establish. Connecting to a culture, an ancestor, or a deity will take time—and that's okay!

One of the most exciting parts (to me) of working with a deity is creating a sacred space or altar for them. This provides you with a place to give offerings, commune with, and recognize the deity in your life and within your reconnection journey. Depending on the culture and tradition, you may have access to shrines, temples, or worship sites that allow you to pray to and give offerings to the divinity you want to work with and a home altar may not be necessary. However, if you are seeking a relationship with a deity of a religion that is not dominant or doesn't have accessible worship sites in your current country, is part of an ancient religion that is only practiced in revival circles, or if you wish to create a home altar in addition to visiting local shrines and temples, then the exercises that follow may help you.

CREATING A DEITY ALTAR

Before creating an altar to a deity, decide on the space that you want it in. This could be in a living room near a hearth for deities of the home, a small altar in the bedroom for deities related to partnership, love, and sex (even if you don't have a partner!), an outdoor altar or a space on an existing altar. I tend to keep my ancestral altars and my deity altars separate due to my recent ancestors being Catholic while I am a devotee of a pre-Christian goddess. After deciding on a space, you can begin the process of setting up an altar. Here are a few steps I utilize in my process of setting up altars:

✥ Clean the space you want to dedicate to your deity with a cleansing or protective water relevant to your tradition, such as four thieves vinegar, rue water, or Florida Water.

✥ Lay down an altar cloth, animal pelt, or protective item to shield the surface you wish to create for your altar. This is an optional step and can be utilized for wood surfaces, windowsills, or any surface you don't want wax to drip on or heat to damage.

✥ If you want to, you can also smoke-cleanse the surface as well as anoint it with devotional oil or holy oil. To anoint the surface, draw a symbol of power (cross or a symbol associated with the deity) or anoint the four corners with oil while dedicating the space to this deity.

Altars can be as complex or as simple as you want. I've known people to have effigies, offerings, and more on their altar while others may just have a candle or an oil in the space for their deity. I have two separate spaces for Diana—one is an outdoor altar and one is a space on my working altar with a statue and a few devotional items to her. Here are a few examples of offerings that can be given to deities:

+ Drinks such as water, tea, or liquor
+ Particular amulets or charms that are associated with the deity
+ Imagery of the deity, such as artistic renditions, figurines, or pictures printed from the internet
+ Herbs that are sacred to the deity or associated with them
+ Particular stones or crystals associated with the deity or that they particularly like
+ Divinatory decks or methods dedicated to the deity (for more on this, see page 145)
+ Traditional offerings given to the deity, such as certain foods, candles, offerings of incense or smoke, or even votive offerings
+ Plants, branches, fresh or dried flowers

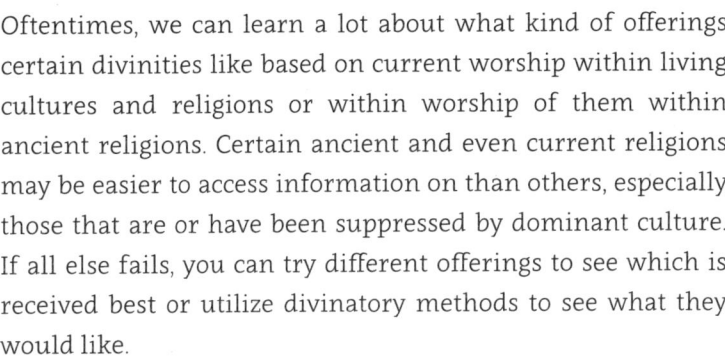

Oftentimes, we can learn a lot about what kind of offerings certain divinities like based on current worship within living cultures and religions or within worship of them within ancient religions. Certain ancient and even current religions may be easier to access information on than others, especially those that are or have been suppressed by dominant culture. If all else fails, you can try different offerings to see which is received best or utilize divinatory methods to see what they would like.

I always like to use a glass-encased prayer candle to begin my deity altars. This could be a color that corresponds with the deity you want to work with and worship or a simple white or black candle. Some of my friends also use screen-printed candles, similar to screen-printed saint candles. I also like to write the name of the deity, symbols associated with them, and even intentions for working with or worshipping them. Below is a ritual I typically use to consecrate and create a candle devoted to a particular deity.

DEVOTING A CANDLE TO A DEITY

Materials:

- Incense associated with the deity you are working with
- A glass-encased candle with a color of your choice or associated with the deity
- Herbs sacred to or associated with the deity (optional)
- An oil associated with the deity or a devotional oil (optional)

Ritual:

1. Light your incense in whatever way is appropriate depending on the type of incense used (cone, stick, or loose).
2. Take your glass candle and hold it over the incense so the smoke engulfs the candle. You can state your intentions for this candle during this time if you wish.

3. Using a Sharpie or paint marker, write the name of the deity you are dedicating the candle to on the side of the glass. You can also add an intention for working with or worshipping the deity and symbols associated with the deity on the candle.

4. If you are using a devotional oil or herbs sacred to your deity, use a long, thin instrument, such as a porcupine quill or a kebab skewer, to carefully poke three to four holes in the candle.

5. Add a small amount of oil to each hole, moving any excess clockwise around the candle.

6. If you are using herbs, you can either grind them up or use them whole. Carefully add a small amount to the top of the candle.

7. Finally, light your candle and set it on the space you have designated as your deity's altar space. During this, you can verbally state your intentions for working with or worshipping the deity.

DEDICATING A DIVINATORY DECK OR SET TO AN ENTITY

Dedicating a form of divination, especially a deck or another set of objects, is a fantastic way of setting a precedent for communication with an entity. Dedicated decks can be anything—a simple card deck, an oracle deck, a traditional tarot deck, a set of runes, or a different divinatory method. Similar to many exercises in this book, dedicating a divinatory deck or set to an entity can be as simple or as complex as you like!

Before you begin, decide which entity you want to dedicate your deck to. This can be a patron god or goddess, or a deity you work with in a more informal context—such as my work with Mercury for particular rituals and spells.

Next, decide on the divinatory deck or set. This could be a particular deck with certain symbolism related to an entity, a deck or set that reminds you of the entity you wish to dedicate it to, or a traditional method of divination to dedicate to the entity. You can use a deck you already own.

If you are feeling insecure about seeking communication with ancestors, a deity, or other spirits, you should only use the deck you have decided is for each entity when asking to commune with them. Below is a ritual to assist you in dedicating a deck to an entity.

Materials:

+ A chime candle in the color of your choice
+ A devotional oil to the entity (optional)
+ An incense blend based on the entity you are devoting your deck to
+ The divinatory deck or set you are devoting to the entity
+ A firesafe or fireproof dish (optional)

Ritual:

1. Begin by carving the name or names of the entity you are devoting the deck to into your chime candle.
2. Anoint the chime candle by rolling it in oil (if using) and a bit of incense blend if it is loose.

3. Light your candle. A verbal incantation can be used if desired.

4. Light your incense or burn it if it is loose incense. This can be done with a charcoal disc in a fireproof dish.

5. Take your divinatory set or deck and hold it over the smoke, allowing the smoke to move around the divinatory deck or set.

6. After cleansing with the incense blend you formulated, begin a reading with the intention of communing with the entity. These questions can be as vague or as complex as needed, but asking about offerings, current and future relationships, and how this entity will come to you through the divinatory deck or set are always great options.

Moving forward, this deck should be kept on an altar space or around the altar space of the entity it's devoted to, and the deck should only be utilized for communicating with this entity.

ANCESTRAL HERBAL ALLIES

In the words of my teacher, Lisa Fazio, "Plants are our ancestors that are still alive." Herbal allies come to us for different things at different times—there are herbal allies that assist us in grief work, healing the heart space, boundaries, and more. For example, olive oil is often used in *mal'occhio* cures all throughout Italy—the olive plant, the fruit of which the oil is made from, is one that my ancestors used again and again as an ally to protect, banish, and cure. Stories of wolves are present throughout Italy, especially the she-wolf who suckled Romulus and Remus and birthed Rome. The Italian wolf is the unofficial national animal, and my ancestors' town even has a statue of a wolf in their open-air museum, built in 1914. La Lupa, the icon of Rome, filtered down into modern-day Italy and the wolves' presence in the Apennine Mountains and Western Alps contributed to a variety of folklore and stories throughout the ages, including the Wolf of Gubbio, the werewolves of Puglia, and more. Both olive oil and leaves as well as the wolf are among my ancestral allies, aiding me in various ways, including curing *mal'occhio* and when it comes to culinary traditions. I even worship the she-wolf, La Lupa, alongside my patron goddess, Diana.

This section makes way for another method of reconnection—food. In many cultures, food is not only something you ingest, but represents tradition, community, and a way of connecting with the people around you. Traditional dishes can also be offerings to those that came before us, such as *pan de muerto*, or Mexican Day of the Dead bread. Plant, herb, and certain animal allies have more to offer us by providing us with sustenance and flavor. You can connect with these ingredients by ingesting them. While you don't need to make food you are uncomfortable with or unable to eat, even adding a sprinkling of an herb that is often found in culinary dishes traditional to your ancestors' homeland allows you to connect with them in greater ways. Including an herb your grandparents or great-grandparents frequently used in a dish you love can allow it to come forward into your life through ingestion—plus you will have some of the dried herb available to work with.

Ancestral plant allies represent culinary, medicinal, and magical herbs that grow in your ancestral lands, were used by your ancestors, or that can help you in your reconnection practice. Certain plants are often utilized more in particular regional practices or cultures depending on the environment the folk are from. In Italy, the usage of herbs in medicine, magic, food, and ritual depends on the region that one is in. While there are particular herbs that are utilized across the country, pre-unification it was likely that our ancestors worked with the plants they found outside their door. In *Italian Magic: Secret Lives of Women*, Karyn Crisis discusses some of the practices of the healers and their formulas. The Aplini sisters, Anna and Maria, utilized a specific herb in one of their cures: "The sisters didn't know the name of the plant, they only knew where to harvest it" (Crisis, 2020), giving an example of this.

For people within rural areas who didn't have access to medicine in the ways we do today, it was necessary to learn the healing, and even the spiritual, properties of herbs—in some places, this is still the way things are done. Herbal medicine and herbal allies allow us not only a physical but a spiritual way of connecting with our ancestors.

To truly connect with our ancestral plant allies, we have to recognize them as living, breathing spirits and those that are teachers to us—they teach us through the way they grow, the way they heal, and the way they interact with us and inform our senses. Plants have been around much longer than we have, and even in this way they can pass us knowledge from their time spent on this planet as a species or even as an individual plant. Mallorie Vaudoise, in her book, *Honoring Your Ancestors*, explains this further: "Ross Heaven writes in *Plant Spirit Shamanism* that 'in Peru, the mother spirit of a plant is the soul of its species. Each plant ... contains its own soul, but it is the combined energy or essence of these leaves that forms the mother.' We might extend this logic a bit and call each physical specimen of a species that we encounter a 'daughter'" (Vaudoise, 2019). The "mother" and the "daughter" may be similar in many ways, but they also may have different lessons. They each have the ability to pass the mother's knowledge to us, but like live mothers and daughters, they may give the knowledge in a slightly different way or tweak it to better fit them.

When I talk about connecting with plants, animals, or spirits in general, I often get a lot of questions about specifics or what this can look like. I'm often asked if I connect with a specific plant spirit growing in a particular time or space or if I'm connecting with the spirit of a plant that exists beyond one singular growth point. Working with the plant or animal ally looks different for everyone—sometimes it means having a live plant within your sacred space, ingesting a flower essence, or working with the dried plant matter. For animals, it could be spending time outside bird-watching, finding ethically sourced bones, or even traveling to nature reserves to learn more about the habitat your animal allies engage with.

With certain plants and animals, this is more difficult. Wolves haven't been spotted in Colorado in years, and while I would love to travel to Italy and familiarize myself with the region of one of my allies, it isn't financially plausible for me at this moment. Seasonality is also a major element when working with both ancestral allies—certain animals receive TV features during specific times of the year, such as the Katmai National Park bear live stream from late July into August, and during shark week when information and features about sharks are plentiful. In connection with my animal allies, I find myself researching their behaviors and their natural environments as well as their spiritual significance.

For herbal allies, I work with primarily dried material and flower essences. I work with my allies to create powders, spiritual waters, teas, and even herbal liqueurs to further work with plant teachers in my life and practice. I am, in many ways, connecting with the whole spirit of rue or rose on a daily basis—but I am also tending to the live plants and energies that I come into contact with, such as the multiflora rose growing in my backyard or the rue that I have been growing for a year and a half. Each plant is a carrier of the lessons that other plants of the same kind hold, yet at the same time each one is slightly different. This allows me the understanding that while I connect with the spirit of rose, each variety of her and even each individual living plant of her has something slightly different to tell me. Here are some ways that we can begin to recognize and connect with our ancestral plant allies:

1. Researching native plants using a database such as iNaturalist to recognize native herbal allies and animals.

2. Referring to books like *Plant Witchery* by Juliet Diaz that concentrate on plants as spirits and provide a guide to connecting with different plant allies. While you may not find all of your ancestral allies within this book, the way it is formatted and the way it talks about allies can assist you in reformatting the way you think about plants and working with them.

3. Researching folkloric charms, cures, and stories about both animals and plants in the region of your heritage—for example, garlic is heavily regarded as a plant/herb of apotropaic qualities in Italy due to its association with Saint Michael the Archangel. Pliny the Elder considered

garlic to be a "cure-all" or panacea, and the uses of garlic in Italian and Italian American culture range from a culinary staple to the hanging of garlic bulbs around the home to ward away *mal'occhio* (the evil eye) or guard against illness. Garlic is even used alongside other apotropaic charms in *breve* bags—"small packets or bags made of fabric and worn around the neck next to the skin" (Magliocco, 2000).

4. Visiting the region of your heritage to learn more about the natural environment and bioregion.

5. Physically acquiring the plant via dried or live specimens, physically acquiring remains of animal allies—after researching native herbal allies and animals, you can begin to connect with them by acquiring dried, live, or dead remains of the plant or animal. This allows you to not only give the plant or animal ally a place of honor in your sacred space, but to begin venerating the plant or animal and calling their presence into your life.

6. Ingesting herbal extracts or flower essences to connect energetically with the plants. Make sure the herbal extracts are made by an herbalist and are safe to ingest, or thoroughly research making your own. Herbs can be processed into different ways of ingesting, such as water extractions like tea and herbal infusions, a tincture through vinegar or wine, a glycerin extraction, or infused oil or honey. Make sure you are fully aware of the effects of ingesting the different types of extractions—some will have no effect and will help you energetically connect with the plant, while others contain parts of the plant that may have effects on your body. Know your allergies, any

possible interactions with medications you are taking, and talk to an herbalist and familiarize yourself with the different extraction methods before trying this. Look into traditional cultural dishes and which plants or herbs are utilized frequently.

7. Exploring folk medicine in your ancestors' homeland. A great way to look into this is by connecting with your community (see page 67) or utilizing research and resources (see page 9). What plants were used for protection? Were there plants that were utilized more frequently?

8. Seeking out teachers or elders that facilitate space to connect with ancestral herbal allies, such as classes, writings, or other resources. Finding ancestral plant allies or identifying them and actually connecting with them are two different beasts. Each practitioner that I've talked to discusses different ways of connecting with a plant. One of my co-workers says his teacher required them to journey to a physical, living plant and meditate with it. My teacher facilitated our connections with ancestral herbal allies through the ingestion of elixirs or flower essences. Different traditions and practitioners give different responses to how to approach plant allies, but there are a few things that are similar which I've implemented into my practice with ancestral plant allies.

RESPECT

To approach a plant as an ally is to approach it on an equal footing. Respecting the plant ally, including respecting receiving a "no" from them when asking for assistance, is key in this aspect of our journey as well as in all forms of spirit work.

RECOGNIZING AUTONOMY

Recognizing the autonomy of a plant spirit is recognizing that it is not something for you to command. This plays out differently in different practitioners' workings with plant allies. For some, this may be asking consent from a plant before communicating with it, asking before gathering/foraging a plant, or even recognizing that the plant's lesson for us may not be something we are ready to receive or like. To recognize plants as autonomous is to acknowledge that their lessons will not abide by what we want to gain from them, but rather what the plant believes will be best for us to learn.

RESTRAINT

To honor plants, not just ancestral allies, but all allies, is also to recognize when a plant is not for us. There are many plants that are commodified, capitalized on, or romanticized for the entire population while they were originally sacred to one specific group in a specific area. Native plants outside our door, although accessible, may not always be for us. Not all plants are made for us to pick or work with, nor do any of the plants that do want to teach us belong to us. To recognize, especially as settlers on stolen land, that we are not entitled to the sacred allies of Indigenous peoples is the key to recognizing our own ancestral and cultural allies. For more about this, see page 123.

Connecting with ancestral herbal allies is, at the center, a decolonization and de-settling of what we believe about plants. To accept plants and herbal allies as teachers is to push back against the narrative of man versus nature and recognize that plants exist not just for our consumption and usage as tools, but live next to us as spirits to be considered before we consume and work with them. It is to acknowledge that we are not always the protagonist or the authority in the battle surrounding the commodification and overuse of plants. It is not always our role to decide where plant allies should be or who they're for.

To respect plant allies, recognize their autonomy, and to exercise restraint is to push back against the teaching that plants do not hold spirits or knowledge past what we have discovered about them. Rather, it is to accept them as elders and recognize that we can learn from them in ways that aren't written about in books or taught in our science lessons.

There are several methods of connecting with plants that have been discussed thus far, but my favorite by far is through the ingestion of the plant via elixir, physical plant, or flower essence. These are different things and may be different depending on the plant. An elixir is not necessarily an official term, but could include the ingestion of a tonic, tincture, or tea that contains plant matter. This could also be a mix of different plant-based formulas, such as a cordial, a syrup, or an *amaro*. A physical plant could be a culinary herb, vegetable, or even the leaves of an edible plant that we can consume to connect with the spirit.

As explained in *Radical Remedies* by Brittany Ducham, a flower essence is by far the most sustainable method of connection with herbal allies because it doesn't necessarily involve any harvesting of the plant. The flower of the ally is dipped in spring water, then diluted to give an essence that contains a subtle, vibrational method of working with a plant ally. Flower essences do not contain any plant material, thus are regarded as one of the safest ways to commune with certain plants, especially if they are poisonous. I most likely prefer this method due to the fact that it is the one my teacher uses to help us connect with and find ancestral herbal allies, and I find that it is my favorite method to commune with plant allies due to its subtle nature.

CONNECTING WITH AN ANCESTRAL ALLY THROUGH FLOWER ESSENCES

If you choose to connect with a plant ally through flower essence, here are a few tips that I utilize when working with flower essences in my practice.

- When you first take the essence, take it in a quiet or sacred space where you can truly feel the plant and how it's connecting to you. Be clear about your intention.

- Be open to the lesson and the plant. If you feel as though it's a harsher lesson, give yourself space to feel it and process it. Adaptability is key during this period.

- Be aware that you may receive a "no" from this ally and be willing to put the essence down and stop consuming it if this is the case.

- Work with the plant every day over a period of seven to nine days. This allows you time to see how the plant is present in your life when you are actively working with it.

- Take notes. Write down how your time is going while engaging with this plant ally. Some ideas for what to write about can include:
  - Your emotional or mental state during the period of working with the essence and plant ally.
  - What kind of dreams you're having, if any.
  - What activities, ideas, and experiences are happening during the ingestion of the flower essence. This could be a feeling of being drawn to certain activities, such as finding that you are more drawn to being outside, research, or creating, or this could even be your response to the people around you.

After the seven- to nine-day period, reflect on your notes with the following questions:

1. What did you experience in your body when you first ingested the flower essence? Did you feel the temperature in your body change at all?
2. What emotions did you experience during the period of working with this plant ally? Do you feel like these emotions are regular in your day-to-day, or do you feel like the ally brought them forward for you?
3. What experiences did you have in liminal spaces during ingesting this plant ally? Did you dream? If so, of what did you dream?
4. During this work with this plant ally, did you feel as though you were revisiting the past, planning your future, or focused on the present?
5. What were your intentions when you brought this plant in to work with? Do you feel like your intentions were met? In what ways did the plant meet your expectations and in which ways did it subvert or change them?
6. What did the plant give you, physically and emotionally? How did this plant change the material world around you?
7. What was the lesson from this plant?

Some of my biggest ancestral plant allies were found through the utilization of flower essences, and because of that, here are some things to watch out for:

✢ You find that during the ingestion of the flower essence, you were receiving everything you needed during that week. This may be patience, assistance in communication, creativity or even roadblocks being moved.

✤ During the ingestion of the flower essence, you feel as though you are going about your normal life. This isn't necessarily not noticing a difference in your day-to-day, but feeling as though the plant immediately began working with you readily and easily to the point where it feels normal and natural.

OTHER METHODS OF CONNECTION

We can also learn about plants by finding out their medicinal properties, their flavor profiles, and how they grow. Below are three separate ways of doing this that allow those who may not have access to flower essences or a physical plant, a way to connect with what ancestral plant allies have to teach us.

MEDICINAL PROPERTIES

Plants heal, harm, and hold different properties that can help us in our day-to-day. I often say that learning the herbalism side of a plant helps us figure out its magical side, and I find that to be true. For example, garlic contains allicin, a strong antibiotic that is released when cloves are crushed or chewed. Garlic cloves have been used medicinally throughout history to fight infection and boost the immune system. Garlic, in Italian American belief, is also a strong protective plant ruled over by Saint Michael the Archangel. Many types of plant allies have medicinal properties, including some which are poisonous if consumed but were used in salves or unguents for chronic pain or particular diseases. Certain types of medicines are even derived from particular poisonous plants.

To research more about medicinal properties of ancestral herbal allies, look into folk medicine in the areas of your ancestral homelands. As well as this, spend time learning from herbalist books or herbalists about the uses for particular plant allies. Medicinal properties of plants can be looked at through different lenses or practices and there is often a different approach in Western medicine versus Eastern medicine in herbalism. Some examples of lenses could include traditional Western herbalism, Ayurvedic approaches, and traditional Chinese herbalism.

CULINARY PROFILES

Certain flavor profiles or scents of plants can assist us in learning about their lessons. In some cases, strong-smelling plants or herbs tend to have magical associations with protection or banishing, such as garlic, mentioned earlier, or asafoetida, also referred to as "devil's dung." Asafoetida is a plant in the ferula family, which includes 220 species. I also find that certain tastes can help us understand the lessons from plants—especially those that are stronger-tasting or have a more nuanced or bitter flavor profile.

For exploring culinary profiles, begin discovering what food tastes like once the plant ally is added or even what the herbs and vegetables taste like by themselves. Begin exploring what the plant ally gives you when you consume it—is it rich in protein? Does it contain certain valuable probiotics that assist you in healing? Is it a stronger-tasting plant or a more neutral-tasting plant? Use the flavor groups of sweet, salty, sour, bitter, and umami to assist you in connecting with this aspect of plant allies.

GROWTH PATTERNS

Plants tell us so much about themselves just by existing. How a plant grows—whether it's vining, what soil it prefers, where it grows—can teach us lessons. The growth of dandelions, despite all odds, can teach us persistence. Begonias, a notoriously picky houseplant, teach us that the things we require to grow in our day-to-day life are a necessity, not the result of neediness.

There's no better way to understand what plants teach us from their growth patterns than by going out and seeking out a plant ally. Spend time in your yard or herb garden watching the way the plant reacts to the environment around it. What do the branches or stems of the ally look like? Is the herb growing upwards, outwards, vining, or all of the above? What kind of soil and environment does it prefer? Does it enjoy full sun, partial sun, or shade? Does it grow in hard-to-reach places? Is it hardy?

Oftentimes, ancestral herbal allies may be plants that you grew up with growing in your garden, utilized in cultural dishes, or got used to seeing hanging around the house. A few of the ancestral herbal allies that I utilize in my practice are listed below, as well as some background information on their herbal medicine uses, regional folk uses, and different cultures that have used them throughout history.

Rose (*Rosa rubiginosa*):
Rose is a well-known herb ally for many practitioners and has a variety of uses. Rose was created, according to Greek mythology, by the goddess of flowers by breathing life into a woodland nymph who had died. Dionysus gave it a beautiful smell, and Aphrodite gave rose her name by rearranging the letters of the name of Eros, the god of desire and love. Roses are thought to be the origin of Catholic rosary beads, and are frequently used in love spells, utilizing the opening of the heart space, and are common funerary flowers. Roses are found in association with many different deities across the world—including the Virgin Mary and different apparitions of her, Aphrodite, Venus, and Freyja, Norse goddess of love. Roses are flowers that represent not only love, but also protection—their stems contain thorns that pierce when touched. Rose is also a flower of death, and is used on burial grounds and in offerings to the dead during funerals. I also personally associate rose with ancestral veneration and worship due to this—it's a grief flower and can be worked with to soothe, heal, and mend. Rose is a gentle, protective teacher—she asks us how we can begin to show up for ourselves, our ancestors, and for others. Rose teaches us about our capacity to love others, but also ourselves. She* asks us how we can protect ourselves, our communities, but also how we can continue ancestral lines and bring forward the intrinsic knowledge that we hold inside of us.

---

* You'll notice that I may refer to plants as she, he, it, or they. Plants, in my opinion, are not gendered, but their associations or our personal experiences with them may allow us to perceive them as more feminine, masculine, non-gendered or androgynous energies. Different practitioners working with plant allies will refer to the same plants by a variety of gendered pronouns, but some plants may have a trend of appearing as the same gendered energy.

Rose syrup recipe:

Rose is one of my most valued allies, and one of the easiest to access. I like to make rose syrup for ingestion and for ritual communion with her.

Materials:

- Water
- A way to heat water
- Red rose petals
- A measuring cup, heat-safe
- Strainer
- White sugar or another sweetener
- A glass jar or container, sterilized

Ritual:

1. Safely heat up the water while prepping one to two cups of red rose petals. I tend to match the amount of water to the amount of rose petals. If I want to make one cup of rose syrup, I use one cup of water and one cup of petals. For two cups of rose syrup, I use two cups.

2. Pour hot water over the rose petals in a heat-safe measuring cup.

3. Set aside to steep for fifteen minutes.

4. After steeping, pour the liquid into the strainer over the jar or container to catch the water. Try to get as much liquid from the petals as possible.

5. Add two parts sugar to the liquid—this would be four cups of sugar for two cups of water or two cups of sugar for one cup of water. Do this while the water is still hot.

6. Stir well, then set aside to cool down.

Rue (*Ruta graveolens*):
Rue is an ally steeped in history and in the culture of both Italian and Italian American practices as well as various Latin American folk practices. Known as the "herb of grace," rue is an herb found in a variety of folk practices for its protective and banishing properties. With antispasmodic, antifungal, and antimicrobial properties, rue has a long history in medicine and magic. They are believed to ward off evil and plague, and is often utilized in amulets, *breve* bags, or is dried and burned. It is frequently placed by doorways to protect a home from evil and was created into brushes to sprinkle holy water before Roman Catholic mass. Legend says that "a rue plant at the foot of the cross was watered by Mary's tears and rue therefore became a symbol of her sorrow and grace" (House of Good Fortune, 2024), giving the plant its folk moniker.

The usage of the herb for righting menstrual cycles and inducing abortion can rightfully link them as an ally to both the Virgin Mary and Diana, as well as other saints and entities associated with childbirth and menstruation. In Italian folk practices, a sprig of rue is depicted on the *cimaruta*, an amulet that is worn for protection or hung above an infant's bed. Each stalk or stem of the amulet contains an apotropaic charm, such as a key, moon, dagger, vervain or rue flower, serpent, or the head of a rooster. There are theories linking the *cimaruta* to Diana, including its depictions of the moon on the end of a branch and the usage of a rue branch by itself. Rue, as an herb, is a fierce protector and associated with solar energies and fire. This is reflected in its medicinal properties by not only the toxicity of the plant and its survival in harsh, hot, climates, but also in its potential to give one phytophotodermatitis—where touching the plant's volatile oils and being exposed to the sun can cause a burning, blistering reaction upon the skin.

Rue's ability to protect us from ailments, evil, and plague while simultaneously harming us if we disrespect them represents their capability as a powerful protector and ally, but also explains their usage in banishing and baneful magics. Rue exists with duality and nuance as a teacher—their lessons tell us to protect, but also to take matters further when necessary. That banishments and justice do not always appear in front of us, but have to be induced by us. Rue is an herb of empowerment, of respect, of both defensive and offensive protection. They demand respect, to thrive in less-than-perfect conditions, and to accept and work with our duality as humans and as reconnectors through both the comfort and the discomfort.

A prayer to rue for protection and her wisdom

> Rue, Herb of Grace, protector against evil,
>   banisher, boundary-setter,
> I pray to you for your protection
>   against mal'occhio, jettature, fatture,
>   and invidia
> From those who may do harm against
>   me or my loved ones,
> Your guidance in {state your current
>   situation or what you are seeking
>   assistance in}.
> I humbly ask for your wisdom and lessons.

Juniper (genus *Juniperus*):
Juniper is a plant that has many different varieties in a vast swath of areas across the world. I originally connected with juniper very early on in my reconnection journey. Later, I learned of juniper's association with the Virgin Mary, its protection from theft, and its nature as a dutiful plant for abundance and cleansing. In legend, the Holy Family was running from Herod's threats. As Mary looked for a place to hide her child, the juniper, filled with small, prickly branches, opened itself up and as she stepped in, she was surrounded by softness. Herod's soldiers passed by unaware, solidifying the story of juniper as a plant of protection from jealousy, threats, and evil as well as its associations with the Virgin Mary as Our Lady's Shelter.

Juniper is also well-known as the flavoring agent in gin and as a plant with various medicinal properties, including aiding digestion, stomach ailments, and for inducing miscarriage. Juniper's wood is aromatic and was used in the ritual purification of temples, a spring-time cleansing, and during outbreaks of plague. Juniper's folklore and usage have been found in Ireland, Scotland, ancient Egypt, and central Europe, while it was also used by various Indigenous Turtle Island tribes including the Cheyenne in ceremony to banish fear of thunder, the Navajo, who burned it to create smoke for hunters, and the Kitasoo, who rubbed sprigs on their backs for good fortune (Miller, 2022).

Juniper's history of medicinal usage has led to its use in modern herbalism for its antiseptic and diuretic properties, while its folklore has led to its continued use within multiple folk magics as a protector and purifier. He is said to banish things injurious to well-being, extending his use from a banisher to an ally that could be petitioned to bring in all that assists, including health, love, and money. His associations with anti-theft extend into protection of money and abundance, as well as protection of the home.

Juniper's lessons are those of protection, boundaries, and tending to our local spirits—inside and outside the hearth. Juniper, as an ally, has the capability to teach us when to be prickly and when to be soft. I find that juniper is a vocal and communicative ally. He tells me when he is frustrated or doesn't want to work with me by pricking my fingers with his sharp needles, and when he's happy to be worked with, am able to handle the plant without being pricked.

Vervain (*Verbena officinalis*):

Vervain, similar to earlier plants, has deep associations with protection and purification. It's called the enchanter's herb, simpler's joy, and holy herb. By many ancient societies, including the Romans and Greeks, vervain was used to protect against evil spells and negative energy, and to purify ritual spaces. However, like some other allies mentioned here, vervain is considered a *panacea* or a cure-all plant—meaning its uses are endless.

Vervain can be used to purify and protect, curse and hex, heal, and bring in luck and love. Its folklore has been influenced by many regions, with various ideas of how it entered into legend—including being used to sweep altars of gods in ancient Rome, being worn for good luck and used as protection for Roman messengers during times of war. It has strong associations with Venus and Isis, and was recommended as an aphrodisiac.

Vervain's importance continued past ancient times into the Christian age, being called the "holy herb" and found at Calvary at the foot of the cross. It was said to have been used to staunch Christ's wounds, and throughout the Middle Ages the profound belief in Vervain's miraculous properties continued—it could heal every wound received in battle and bring about immortality to heroes (June, 2020). Vervain's medicinal properties are rich. It is a nervine, a plant remedy, and is often recommended for relaxing the nervous system, but it is also considered diaphoretic, an expectorant, hypotensive, sedative, astringent, a digestive bitter, antispasmodic, and more.

Vervain continues to be an important magical herb today, finding its way into *The Witching Herbs* by Harold Roth alongside rue and also in countless blogs and plant ally studies. Vervain, while being a potent medicinal and magical ally, is also fantastic ecologically—bees, wasps, butterflies, and flies treat it as a nectar source and it can be eaten by multiple larvae as well as songbirds. Vervain teaches us a variety of things in its lessons, and I've found, like all herbal allies, but especially panacea plants, that the lesson will be incredibly specific to the practitioner and the individual learning from it. For me, vervain is a teacher of how the mundane and the magical intertwine, how we hold the duality of love and fear of the unknown inside all of us.

Chamomile (*Matricaria chamomilla*):

I first stumbled upon chamomile as an ancestral ally in "The Indigenous Healing Tradition in Calabria, Italy" where it was listed for its usage for calming anxiety in the form of a tea. In folklore, chamomile is considered the sun's herb, its flowers golden and numerous. Chamomile is included in a miscellaneous collection of Anglo-Saxon medical texts as one of the "Nine Sacred Herbs." The Greeks noted it for its strong and delicious aromatics and Frances A. Bardswell noted its "remarkable effect on other plants" (Bardswell, 1911), calling it the "plant's physician" and it's said to not only improve the health of nearby plants, but their growth as well. In ancient Egypt, the plant was considered "a gift from the divine ... offerings of the flower were made to the ... sun god Ra ... the plant's oil was used to anoint the dead ..." (Lui McKinnon, 2023). Chamomile is most likely thought to be effective against evil spirits for its fragrance, considering that, "When the miasma theory was still popular, pomanders and pleasant-smelling herbs were credited with keeping disease at bay" (Marble Crow, 2020).

Similar to other plants listed here, chamomile is considered a panacea or a "cure-all." It has the ability to help and heal in many magical and medicinal practices, as well as having historical associations of being used for luck, sleep, purification, protection, prevention against negativity, and sometimes even banishing. As a flower with Roman, German, or even English variations, chamomile is found and utilized differently all over the world, depending on who you ask.

In my tradition, chamomile is both an healing herb and an attraction herb—I associate it strongly with the energy of the sun. As a solar herb, it assists in confidence, drawing of luck, protection from evil, and calming. I often drink it in tea during cold seasons mixed with marshmallow root and utilize it in money and luck workings. As an ally, chamomile is playful and abundant. It reminds me frequently of the Sun card in the tarot, an exploration of our relation to our inner child while also remaining protective of that contentment and joy.

Pine (*Pinus*):
Pine is a newer ally that I work with, and a strong ancestral one. Pine trees exist in a variety of places and regions around the world, with deep folklore in each place it pops up. Near my ancestral hometown lies La Sila, a mountainous plateau and national park filled with pine trees. La Sila influences local cuisine with very specific flavours and ingredients, and with processing and storage of food. The region itself has a particular variety of pine—Pino della Sila or *Pinus laricio*, mentioned in writings by Strabo, Norman Douglas, Gertrude Slaughter, and more.

Pine's folklore spreads from Sweden to Italy and everywhere in between. Mentions in ancient Greek mythology link pine to Rhea and Pitys, a nymph punished by Boreas for preferring Pan over him. Pine trees have been used for protection by numerous cultures across the globe including making crosses from the needles to keep evil away, burning to return curses to the sender, and nailing branches to doors to keep those with bad intentions out (Sedgwick, 2022). Pine's cones and those of other conifer trees are well-known to be used as decoration for wreaths, trees, and the like for winter celebrations, such as Christmas or the solstice, and evergreen represents immortality and rejuvenation during some of the longest nights of the year. Evergreens are heavily associated with the god Baldr, who rules over light and peace, in the Norse pagan tradition. The Romans marked the winter solstice with the festival of Saturn, a god of agriculture, and brought evergreen boughs to decorate their homes.

The evergreen is also well-known for its medicinal usage of rubbing its oil on the skin to lower nerve pain or as a tincture to fight respiratory infections or colds. Pine is another plant whose protection against disease correlates to protection magically. Its cones can represent prosperity and blooming, while its needles and resin can represent healing and security. As a plant ally, pine's lessons are stability, strength, and conservation. It provides shelter and food to a large variety of wildlife, while also giving us the gift of its resin to help us heal our wounds. Pine asks us what we can do to protect our homes, find light in the dark, and bring stability and strength into our practices.

Garlic (*Allium sativum*):

Garlic is an incredibly important plant in Italian and Italian American folk magic. Associated with Saint Michael the Archangel, its roots as a medicinal and magical ally run deep. Folklore around garlic touts its protection from vampires, devils, and the evil eye. Hanging garlic in the home can protect newborns. Garlic braids over or near a door bring good luck, while repelling thieves and envious people. According to Pliny the Elder, garlic and onions were invoked as deities by ancient Egyptians. Culpeper, an herbalist, links garlic with Mars, a fiery and fierce planet associated with the god of war.

In Italian folk medicine, garlic is linked to the alleviation of stomach aches by putting a poultice on the stomach, or is used to protect from colds by wearing a string of garlic around the neck. It was mentioned by Hippocrates as a recommendation for infections, wounds, and digestive disorders. It is antiseptic, antibacterial, and antifungal and is considered to help boost and improve the immune system, possibly leading to its usage in fire cider, an holistic remedy and tonic made to enhance immunity and help with digestion.

Garlic supposedly contains Saint Michael's essence—it is a fiery warrior and a protector from a slew of things. Garlic, in Italian and Italian American folk magic, is hung over doors, used in protective spells, their peels burned for banishment, and utilized in almost every dish you can think of coming from Italy. Its medicinal benefits are well-known to those who relied on its magic and allyship for health and protection from evil disease and led to garlic's wide usage within cuisine, medicine, and metaphysical workings. As an ally, garlic is stubborn. It's full of fire and will heat your body up when eating it. In protective workings, I've found garlic to feel very natural as an ally to call upon for banishments and more intense workings. Garlic is also the plant I work with the most as an extension of Saint Michael. When ingesting a clove or a flower essence, I recite a folk prayer to the archangel, and it is in this that I find it easiest to communicate with him. Like rose and rue are extensions of Mary and Diana, garlic is that for Saint Michael.

However, you don't need to work with an archangel in order to recognize the power that garlic has across cultures as an apotropaic ally. Similar to rue, too much garlic can be harmful for your body and immune system—representing a trend with our most protective plants also holding the capability to poison us and harm us if they aren't well researched and treated with respect.

Folk prayer to Saint Michael

Michael to the right of me,
Michael to the left of me,
Michael above me,
Michael below me,
Michael within me,
Michael all around me,
Michael, with your flaming sword
Of cobalt blue, please protect me.

Rosemary (*Rosmarinus officinalis*):
Another important herb in my tradition, rosemary is representative of "remembrance" in Victorian flower language, and is often helpful in clearing brain fog and helping with memory. A strong, aromatic herb, rosemary has long been associated with energizing the mind, revitalization, and stimulation. It was often used in love spells during the Middle Ages, including stuffing a poppet with rosemary to attract a lover. In ancient Greece, scholars would wear garlands of rosemary to help with their examinations. It was used as incense during religious ceremonies in Rome, and was, like many other herbs here, used as protection from evil spirits. It is often associated with the sun, the cult of Aphrodite, as well as the Virgin Mary, and it's said that smelling rosemary on Christmas Eve will mean your next year is filled with blessings.

Like other plants that hold duality in their meanings, rosemary is no different. Despite her associations with love and weddings, she is also associated with death and immortality. Rosemary's strong associations with remembrance and usage in funeral rites, including being carried by mourners, solidified her relationship with ancestor work, grief work, and protection during grief. Rosemary's strong scent and ancient theories around miasma mean she is often utilized during times of illness or around the dead (Sedgwick, 2022). In modern practice, rosemary sprigs or bundles are often burned for cleansing and protecting the space, used in a variety of recipes, and sometimes found in recipes for four or seven thieves vinegar, (a spiritual recipe/tonic found in many cultures that is used to protect against the plague and other evils).

As an herbal ally, rosemary's energy always feels strongly linked to the Virgin Mary for me. She is a protective ally, but she is also an ally of the ancestors. While rue and garlic bring fierceness to protection, rosemary often feels softer, kinder, and more gentle in protective rites. She is one of my ancestral allies that is always on my altar spaces and I use her sprigs, dried or fresh, to cook nourishment, burn, and in oils dedicated to communication with spirits. She is a force of balance, representing life, love, and death, and helps us reflect upon our mortality and the ways in which we continue our lineage and how. Rosemary's lessons include reflection, contemplation, and being a better ancestor—her associations with memory and the mind often encourage me to slow down and think before I act and to make space for ancestral veneration in my everyday life.

Fennel (*Foeniculum vulgare*):
As a child, my mother's garden always contained fennel, basil, tomatoes, and oregano. Fennel sat in a small cement planter in our backyard, and grew tall. It sprouted many leaves, and I remember thinking how similar they looked to hair. Fennel has a strong taste, like anise, and her seeds are frequently used in *amaro* as well as protective rites against the evil eye. Pliny the Elder believed that snakes ate fennel to improve their eyesight, leading to his recommendation of using fennel to treat a variety of ailments, including formulas to induce miscarriage and improve the sight. Fennel acts as a uterine stimulant and is well-known for its digestive assistance, often being found in the form of tea or digestive bitters. It is found in the Anglo-Saxon Nine Herbs charm, touted as protection against pain, poison, "fiend's hand," spells, and enchantment. Magically, it purifies spaces when burned and protects from the evil eye, and it is mentioned in certain folk sayings, such as "eye, evil eye, parsley and fennel." An old

prayer to fennel mentions Santa Lucia, whose association with the plant runs deep. Certain treats given to her on her feast day, such as Occhi di Santa Lucia, can be studded with the plant. Santa Lucia is the patron of those with eyesight problems, and she is often petitioned for protection from the evil eye. Fennel's long-standing association with eyesight, and the fact that its seeds resemble eyes, means many prayers to either the plant or the saint tend to also include the other.

Fennel's long stalks were said to be used as staffs, and Pliny believed that fennel, when ingested, would purge/purify the entire body. It was used as a spice, medicine, a calmer of nerves, and insect repellent by ancient peoples, and the Jewish population of Sicily contributed many fennel-based dishes to Sicilian culture. In Tuscany, fennel was served at the end of meals to freshen the breath and aid with digestion. Fennel as a digestive plant and its usage in medicinal and magical recipes to aid with these things provides another link to protective plants in Italian American culture often guarding against both disease and magical attack, representing the intertwining of medicine for the people with the belief of things like the evil eye.

I find fennel to be a very mercurial plant ally—it has many leaves and many seeds. Fennel assists me in opening roads for magical work, carrying messages, and dispelling evil. It's a frequent and constant herb utilized in my *breve* bags, and it always has a prayer to Santa Lucia recited over it beforehand. I find that even carrying fennel with me allows me to tap into the energy of being one of many. Fennel's lessons include communal protection, clarity in the dark, and getting in touch with the intrinsic knowledge we carry in our guts as living ancestors.

An important safety note:
Before consuming any unfamiliar herbs or herb material, please talk to either a licensed doctor or herbalist and check for any interactions that the herb may have with any current medication you are on.

"When we think about plants, we must understand them as complex personalities, just like the people in our lives. No one person is solely identified with one label" (Vaudoise, 2019).

PUTTING IT INTO PRACTICE/EVERYDAY CONNECTION

Accessible right now:
Using a free database or free academic articles to learn more about the ecosystem of your ancestors' homeland as well as particular plants and animals that were important to them. This can expand further into learning about folk medicine from free databases, academic articles, reading blogs, and following teachers that prioritize discussing plant allies in reconnection. Many of your ancestral plant allies may be available to you through certain markets or even the grocery store, whether in live or dried form, allowing you to bring their physical presence into your reconnection practice.

Middle ground:
Creating an ancestral garden and tending to it. For those who don't have access to a yard or a green space, you can utilize a pot on a windowsill or on a balcony. An ancestral garden is a space full of ancestral plant allies and your own personal

plant allies. This is more of a summer project depending on the ancestral allies you wish to connect with, and takes a lot of planning and time to gather the seeds or young plants. Some of the herbal allies present in my ancestral garden are verbena, yarrow, rosemary, rue, basil, and chamomile. All of these herbs have important roles in my practice and in Italian American folk magic.

Investment:
A pilgrimage to your ancestors' homeland to connect with the local flora and fauna. When doing this, it's important to not only prioritize the knowledge of local guides but learn from them rather than act as a tourist on the homeland. Certain teachers and facilitators may plan these pilgrimages, such as Radici Siciliane, while otherwise you may have to seek out mentors and teachers local to the area.

ANCESTRAL PRACTICES

Ancestral practices are an element of your reconnection journey that, similar to me, may be the reason you began your reconnection journey in the first place. I often heard about my nana's novena or the way most of our family was "a little witchy" (my mother's words, not mine!) and that, ultimately, was what spurred my interest and push into reconnecting with Italian American culture. The truth is that reconnection can happen for a variety of reasons. You may have found your family's culture and practices embarrassing when you were younger and pushed yourself away from it only to return to it later in life. You may have felt isolated or excluded and sought out community and culture with people sharing your same background. Reconnection is a personal process that requires us to look at the ways in which we seek community, belonging, and ancestral and cultural reclamation. Ancestral practices allow us to dig a little deeper into the more superstitious, spiritual, or even practical areas of our lineage.

Defining ancestral practice can be different for every practitioner. Here are a few things that are a part of both my personal practice and my ancestral practice and belief system which have influenced my reconnection journey:

- Belief surrounding *mal'occhio* or the evil eye, including how to avoid it, protection against it, how to heal it, and how we act through the belief in it
- Amulets, apotropaic charms, and rituals surrounding them
- Cleansing and keeping a clean house
- Relationships with and around ancestors and spirits, such as plants and saints
- Cooking, including how to receive recipes and which food is good for which occasion
- Rituals for when someone is sick or injured
- Different divinatory methods
- Rituals surrounding holidays, such as the summer solstice, the Epiphany, and Christmas
- The usage of prayers or vernacular healing methods to assist against various ailments, both spiritual and physical

Ancestral folk traditions define themselves, similar to the rest of your reconnection, through community and the folk. They, like the people they serve, work and operate practically. This doesn't mean that it isn't, in itself, spiritual, but oftentimes the traditions and rituals centered around a particular folk magic will reflect the issues needing to be solved to help the people.

In Italian folk magic, this plays out in folk medicine and remedies in the South of Italy where doctors were more inaccessible or too expensive—rather than going to a doctor, people would oftentimes go to see a healer. When doctors became more available in South Italy, this didn't necessarily change—sometimes healers would recommend a client to a doctor, or a doctor would recommend a client to a healer if they felt that the problem was more spiritual than physical. Many spiritual ailments in Italy were linked to very real and physical issues—epilepsy, malaria, fever, and shingles were attributed to *jettatura* (intentional evil eye), while loss of breast milk (milk theft) was attributed to *mal'occhio* (evil eye/jealousy). The cures for these spiritual ailments will often include herbs and methods that will actually work to relieve the pain or symptoms of the illness, such as certain herbs being ingested or applied to the skin. Olive oil mixed with plaster is a remedy in Calabria (cited by an anthropological study written by Stanley Krippner, Ashwin Budden, Roberto Gallante, Michael Bova) for second-degree burns, while olive oil is also used in a common cure for the evil eye. While Sicily uses a particular seaweed grown off its coast for certain rituals, towns in Italy further away from the ocean will use plants found in their bioregion. These often coincide with plants given importance for healing and protective properties in ancient Greece and Rome—not just because of the similar climate, but because this knowledge has in many ways been passed down through generations. Italian folk practitioners may not cite Pliny or other ancient Greek naturalists when referring to horehound, chamomile, mallow or vervain as a cure-all, but they have proverbs about the plants and know they will heal all manner of ailments both spiritual and physical.

Ancestral practices and folk magic rely on the people, the culture, and the materials accessible to the practitioner and the folk in order to function, and oftentimes our ancestral practices may extend beyond what is considered folk magic. The cooking of particular foods at certain times of the year or for different reasons isn't necessarily folk magic, but it is entrenched in our ancestral practices and ways of being. Learning activities that your ancestors did, such as making certain types of drinks, listening to certain music or participating in certain holidays and celebrations, makes room for our ancestral ways of being. This only begins to touch on certain aspects of your ancestors' culture and heritage that can be explored. Ancestral practices and learning about them are also important because, similar to so many other aspects in your reconnection journey, certain things may require a particular method of entry or initiation. This could include particular religious traditions, such as in Judaism or Vodoun, but could also be smaller vernacular traditions, similar to my family's rituals around meatballs (see more on page 111).

When we are able to recognize ancestral practices, whether they are vernacular traditions, folk magics, or initiatory traditions that our ancestors followed, we are able to reconnect and reconstruct things that our family may have lost connection to and catch threads that have been left behind in our day-to-day lives. Connecting to ancestral ways of being and practices allows us to recognize what has been lost, culturally and spiritually, from our family.

Implementing ancestral practices may look different for everyone. Sometimes, information surrounding ancestral practices may be limited or nearly impossible to find. You may only know about your ancestral practices from the limited information left behind from your family, stories from relatives, or even what you can learn from academic sources and other practitioners. Learning about ancestral practices begins at the root and connecting with your ancestors, those that are living and those that are not. To see more on how to build an ancestor altar, see page 105. Similar to other methods described throughout this book, reconnecting with an ancestral practice could be as simple as beginning to incorporate it in your life—like cooking a certain food or celebrating a certain holiday—or as complex as seeking out mentors, initiates, or members of a tradition that you feel is important to your family. For some, it may include the making of certain dishes during particular holiday seasons, like the baking of *grispelle*, a traditional Calabrian Christmas donut, or the baking of *pan de muerto* for those reconnecting with cultures that celebrate *Día de los Muertos*. For others, it may be learning how to make an ancestral dish, like baking challah. A friend of mine celebrated reconnection by seeking out the local mambo of the Haitian Vodou tradition and reaching out to them. It could even be celebrating the Epiphany or researching certain Christmas saints or spirits and giving devotion to them, like Santa Lucia of both Sicilian and Nordic practices and Krampus of German belief.

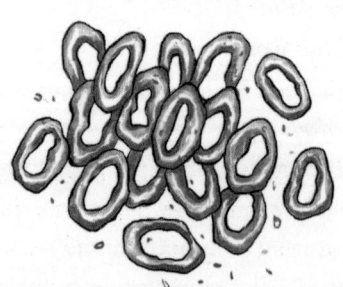

Is folk magic witchcraft?

The answer to this question will be different depending on who you ask—for me, I have never considered some aspects of what I do witchcraft while others certainly are. I tend to try to delineate between which areas of my practice are witchcraft and which are folk magic, especially by calling myself both an Italian American folk practitioner and a folk witch. Both aspects of my life and practice are informed by my Italian American-ness, but not everything that I do is something directly out of my ancestral practices—and that's okay. Reconnection is in part finding what labels and practices work for you.

Many folk practitioners will also consider themselves witches today while knowing their grandma, great-grandma, or great-great-grandma would never use that term to refer to themselves—they had a completely separate word for it and equating it to witchcraft would be, in many ways, doing a disservice to the practitioners and the practice itself. It's because of the history of folk magic and witchcraft that I tend to make this distinction. What I do and what my family before me did is not witchcraft, it is just what we do and did.

In history, witches were persecuted, discriminated against, and singled out. The individual who was sending jettature would often be considered a witch, and many protections in folk magics function to protect against witches, or those who send hexes, curses, and more. Culturally we know that certain rituals, ways of being,

> and more were frowned upon due to their association with witchcraft or the fact that they harmed others—this is reflected across many other countries and areas in Europe. In my family, my grandma and great-grandma did not consider themselves witches, but rather devout Catholics who may have known how to divine certain things or known what to cook to bring luck, love, or prosperity into someone's life.
>
> In the modern day, we know that witchcraft is not something that is inherently bad or wrong and that it does not exist solely to harm others. Witchcraft is an umbrella term that refers to a variety of practices and ways of being. Due to the ways in which folk practices and witchcraft have been at odds with each other historically, the delineation between folk magic and witchcraft in conversations continues to be something that I, as a practitioner of both, do, despite calling myself a mix of both. However, many witches, especially those working within the parameters of both folk magic and witchcraft, blend the terms or utilize terms that they feel comfortable with.

HEALING GENERATIONAL TRAUMA AND LINEAGE

When we start the journey of reconnecting, we are taking on the responsibility of healing generational trauma, lineage, and unsettling settler colonial ideas of race, ethnicity, culture, and white supremacy that we have taken on as part of the process of assimilation. Many of our ancestors were people who owned slaves, put themselves on a pedestal above people of color, and contributed to white supremacy. This work is not new, and it's already been done and continues to be done by Black, Indigenous, and people of color every day. W.E.B. Du Bois, Ta-Nehisi Coates, bell hooks, and more have been discussing the way in which whiteness and anti-Blackness as a social construct and identity is a pervasive factor in today's society as well as how it originated alongside the religious identity of a Christian that was "crucial for the development of the English slave trade" (P. Baird, 2021). Whiteness and the concept of whiteness as an identity was crucial to secure the labor of Africans by positioning slave owners as better than those who were enslaved. It allowed a moral superiority that justified the horrors that were perpetrated against enslaved peoples and, "The idea of whiteness, in other words, was identical to the idea of white supremacy" (Baird, 2021). The social construct of whiteness allowed for homogeneity, uniformity, and power to enslave, murder, colonize, antagonize, insult, and even commit genocide all for the sake of being "better than".

Whiteness creates a society that operates on racial identity, forces assimilation into this identity, and strips individuals of their cultural heritage. Those who maintain a connection to their culture may find that they are faced with discrimination due to their heritage and cultural connections. Reconnecting to and sometimes reconstructing cultural identity is in many ways rejecting the belief that our identity is purely racial—rather, it may have been intrinsically intertwined with our culture over time, as is the case with Black Americans. It is deconstructing and analyzing the ways in which we contribute to white supremacy as well as the ways our ancestors contributed to it. Even in researching ancestry, "white people from privileged backgrounds have a distinct advantage. Forced relocation, immigration, and premature death all blot out the histories of families of color" (Anti-Racism Daily, 2022). Understanding the politics of history, and how even reconnecting with ancestral roots is in many ways racialized, is a way in which we can take accountability for our ancestors who did harm to others. It's also a way in which we, as white people and people with privilege assimilated into harmful ideologies like classism, racism, and more from a young age, can move forward and ally ourselves with people of color. Anti-Racism Daily writes in "Tracing your Ancestral Roots is Easy When You're White": "those who can trace back their family histories should reflect on what those histories mean: their ancestors were the beneficiaries of a system that erased the existence of so many others" (A-RD, 2022).

Reconnection also deconstructs our habit of taking things that are not ours. It allows us space to slow down and consider why we want to practice or utilize something as well as whether or not it is even okay to utilize or practice it in the first place. My teacher, Lisa Fazio, writes of reconnection: "I also believe that, for those of us descended from Europe, our reclamation of our connection to our ancestors and original homelands is an act of transformative justice. When we know who we are, where we are from, and what our relationship is to where we live we can begin to acknowledge our complicity in oppressive and violent colonial systems and recognize our own inherited and intrinsic wealth of medicine and magic. This mitigates and deconstructs the habitual and conditioned impulse to culturally appropriate and colonize the medicine and magic of others and informs the regeneration of being authentic and just belonging, place-making, and cultural emergence" (Fazio, 2019). We can utilize ideas we discussed in our ancestral plant ally section (see page 147) in a similar way when we are looking at practices and traditions we are reconnecting to—respect, recognizing autonomy, and restraint. When we are respecting other cultures, we are automatically switching the narrative that white supremacy upholds—that we are free to colonize, take, and momentarily benefit from art, practices, and areas of significance from cultures we are not accepted into. Recognizing autonomy allows us to understand that the voices, leadership, and freedom of each individual within their culture matters as they are not a monolith. Finally, restraint is the physical action of deciding when an ancestral herbal ally, practice, or ancestral way of being is not ours to utilize or appropriate and actually taking that action to say no.

Accountability in this practice moves past deconstructing whiteness and reconnection with ethnic ways of being, but it is healing the intergenerational trauma that our ancestors as immigrants have experienced. Several theories exist around the way genetic memory recollects our predecessors' environments, experiences, and hardships through epigenetics, or the study of inherited changes in gene expression. These studies indicate that "survivors of traumatic events may have effects in subsequent generations" (Javelosa, 2016). This theory not only expands our knowledge of hereditary genetic traits, but also looks at the way our very fabric of being changes and holds memories from our ancestors. Healing that trauma and experiencing the grief and loss that assimilation and immigration causes is an integral part of reconnection. We cannot heal the pain without first recognizing it and feeling it firsthand. What did it feel like for your ancestors to leave their community and country? What did they experience as they assimilated and felt discrimination for their culture, skin color, or ways of living? How is reconnection with these ways of being healing for us and them?

Accountability is recognizing that many things can be true at once and all of these things coalesce in different ways for different people. It is recognizing our own journey and the culpability and role we are each playing in unsettling settler colonial narratives of white supremacy, cultural homogeneity, and our own lineage healing. It is recognizing the narratives we and our ancestors have contributed to and recognizing the ways in which we as reconnectors can change this for our descendants.

Accountability is not just an individual and personal effort, but a communal one. Recognize that your community should hold you accountable. This may not necessarily be someone you are friends with or a teacher, but another member of the culture you are reconnecting to who is pointing out a bias or a flawed belief that you continue to hold that directly contributes to a problematic way of thinking. Accountability is not something that is pretty or is achieved overnight; it requires the effort of self-reflection, trust, and those around you to hold you to your word and your path as you continue to reconnect. This, in many ways, is why I do not recommend creating community or seeking out community that holds the exact same opinions as you. I don't necessarily mean seeking out those whose intrinsic morals, ethics, and ways of being directly contradict yours, but rather finding teachers, peers, and people within the culture that live different lives and hold different beliefs. Disagreements allow us to analyze our own thoughts and reconnection processes in a way that we may not have access to within a bubble—even if it's frustrating or painful. Many of the disagreements I've had with peers led me to look at my beliefs and ways of thinking around the topic and reform them to better reflect the culture I am reconnecting with.

What is assimilation?

Assimilation, according to some, is a "benign step toward social peace and harmony". Peter Skerry, fellow at the Institute for Advanced Studies in Culture at the University of Virginia, writes, "If you were to ask the average person on the street what is meant by 'assimilation,' he or she would say something about immigrants fitting into American society without creating undue problems for themselves or for those already here" (Skerry, 2000).

Assimilation can occur in many different places and has happened throughout history, but the history of immigration in the United States and the UK has given way

> to more contemporary literature focused on assimilation in these countries. In the United States, for the "first part of the twentieth century, new immigrants were encouraged to 'Americanize' in order to achieve social stability and economic success." In certain terms, it was believed that "cultural homogeneity would lead to less conflict between groups as they came together under one belief system." While assimilation has not always held a negative connotation, with the level of xenophobia that immigrating individuals may face and the extent to which they face it, immigrants are in many ways forced to leave behind cultural heritage and become part of the homogeneity, with Stanford University even reporting that, "Children with less-foreign-sounding names completed more years of schooling, earned more, and were less likely to be unemployed than their counterparts whose names sounded more foreign. In addition, they were less likely to marry someone born abroad or with a foreign-sounding name. These patterns held even among brothers within the same family. The data suggests that, while a foreign-sounding name reinforced a sense of ethnic identity, it may have exposed individuals to discrimination at school or on the job" (Abramitzky, 2017). This same study argues that assimilation is sure to happen, and that "the evidence is clear that assimilation is real and measurable," with people leaving behind their "old ways of life." While assimilation may have been clearly defined in the early twentieth century, it's now a term that has been perforated by contradiction. What even is assimilation? What does it mean to assimilate?
>
> Skerry provides a version of what has historically

been defined as assimilation in America: "First, they had to accept English as the national language. Second, they were expected to live by what is commonly referred to as the Protestant work ethic (to be self-reliant, hardworking, and morally upright). Third, they were expected to take pride in their American identity and believe in America's liberal democratic and egalitarian principles" (Skerry, 2000).

Laila Lalami in her 2017 article "What Does it Take to 'Assimilate' in America?" studies the idea of assimilation further, musing, "For some, assimilation is based on pragmatic considerations, like achieving some fluency in the dominant language, some educational or economic success, some familiarity with the country's history and culture. For others, it runs deeper and involves relinquishing all ties, even linguistic ones, to the old country" (Lalami, 2017).

Lalami discusses the different beliefs of assimilation, everything from "a matter of principle emphasizing a belief in the constitution and the rule of the law; in life, liberty, and the pursuit of happiness; and in a strong work ethic and equality" to "nothing short of the abandonment of all traces of your heritage will do". She discusses how the "perception that visible signs of religious identity are indicators of deep and sinister splits in society that can lead to rabid fears of wholly imaginary threats. Several states have passed anti-Shariah measures, in fear that Muslims will seek to impose their own religious laws on unsuspecting Americans" (Lalami, 2017).

Lalami explores the way in which power dynamics play a role in this—how her home country of Morocco never lamented around how French immigrants contradict local norms, but in France, politicians express outrage that those "descended from North African immigrants choose halal food options for school lunches or want to attend classes in head scarves."

In America, there is no way of truly judging when someone has assimilated, leaving immigrants and descendants of immigrants to flounder and face discrimination or argue in favor of assimilation as it guarantees them safety in whiteness, as it did for Italian and Irish American immigrant populations. What we fail to recognize is that the way of life of many nations, including America, does not center on a specific culture, rather it centers on the racial identity of whiteness and presents those who are people of color, no matter how long they have existed in the United States, as other.

Assimilation is a term that will mean something different for everyone reading this book. For me, it was my ancestors assimilating into whiteness and leaving behind their culture, language, and heritage in order to fit in. For others, it may be a push away from cultural norms that their family has kept or growing up in a migrant home never speaking their ancestors' language. Assimilation may mean becoming a part of the workforce and political sphere or even distancing themself from their familial culture to avoid bullying and discrimination as they grow up. It is, in many ways, a way that "native" Americans, despite originally being settlers and displacing Indigenous communities across Turtle Island, assert themselves over those that they deem and judge as other for racial or cultural reasons.

CREATING SPACE FOR GRIEF

Grief is an important part of the reconnection process that is often overlooked or not talked about—it's common to have a sense of mourning, loss, and grief around aspects of culture that have been lost through assimilation. This exercise allows you to slow down, take a deep breath, and recognize grief as part of the journey you are on.

Materials:

+ A quiet place
+ A mullein torch with a fireproof vessel (optional)
+ A glass of water
+ A notebook and pen

Ritual:

1. Find a quiet place. Make sure this is a place you feel safe and secure in and that you are either alone or with someone to support you through this process.

2. Light your mullein torch if you have it. Make sure it is placed in a fireproof vessel containing water to catch any sparks.

3. If you've lit a torch, as it burns, focus on the following journal prompts. Or, if you've opted not to use a torch, set a timer for yourself to take dedicated time to focus on them. These prompts are optional and may not be applicable to everyone:

- What resentment am I holding onto on this reconnection journey, and towards whom? How can I recognize this resentment as an important part of this process?
- What am I grieving right now? What things have I or my family lost due to whiteness and white supremacy?
- In what ways have I or my family contributed to white supremacy and other structures of power? How am I changing that narrative moving forward?
- In what ways did my ancestors, by force or by choice, forfeit their culture and cultural ways of being? In what ways do I mourn these losses?
- How does my journey as a reconnector differ from that of others? Do those differences make me feel uncomfortable or "less than", especially if they were raised with more remnants of their culture?

Mullein torches

Verbascum thapsus, or mullein, is a native plant to the Mediterranean, Asia, and Northern Africa, and folk names include "Jupiter's staff," "Adam's flannel," "Aaron's Rod," and many others. Mullein torches, also known as hag's torches, are created when mullein's second-year stalk is in full bloom, by gathering and drying the stalks and then dipping them in beeswax. These torches were used by the Romans in funeral processions and mullein was mentioned not only by Pliny the Elder, but in Greek legend where the gods gave Ulysses a mullein stalk to defend himself against Circe (DeBray, 1978). Mullein is regarded as one of the most helpful herbs for respiratory support, and on the Root Circle, Lisa Fazio writes: "Our lungs are the seat of our grief. Grief is one of our most precious living emotions. Grief is one of the gifts of being alive and it is in our lungs that we gather it to be breathed into and inspirited by the elemental matrix we call air" (Fazio, 2018). Mullein and mullein torches provide a way into the emotions that sit on our chest, allowing us to release, observe, and make space for our mourning. The leaves of mullein are emollient, known for softening and soothing, and when inhaled or consumed in tea they are known to moisten the lungs by bringing water into dried-out tissues to release stagnant secretions. Alongside the plant's medicinal uses, mullein does similar things with our emotions and our grief. It helps us to let go of stagnancy, open ourselves up, and then helps us release.

PART 4

TRADITION

Tradition is a word that may induce some discomfort in readers, and that's something to acknowledge. Many times, someone will tell you to do something or that something is morally wrong and their justification is "it's tradition" or "it's just the way it is." Truthfully, traditions can be both beneficial and detrimental. Racism and sexism are traditions that have withstood the test of time, and yet they are a detriment to society. Nowadays, many individuals are moving away from justifying a practice by referencing its historical nature. Instead, they are focused on thinking about the way traditions affect others and dismantling the propensity to utilize the idea that something should remain prominent simply because "that's the way it's always been done." In this book, I will not be offering excuses for detrimental practices simply because they are "traditional." However, I will argue for the importance of both tradition and reconstruction, the ability to analyze our traditions to weed out problematic features, and the capability as reconnectors to not only utilize what our ancestors did, but create something new as well.

THE IMPORTANCE OF TRADITION

Traditions can be seen as many things. According to Merriam-Webster, tradition has several meanings. One of which is "an inherited, established, or customary pattern of thought, action, or behavior." Another is "the handing down of information, beliefs, and customs by word of mouth or by example from one generation to another without written instruction." By these standards, tradition is a term that can be used to define a plethora of things. Tradition could be the way your family or culture celebrates certain holidays or how a particular food dish is cooked. It could be societal beliefs, ideas around faith, or how to conduct oneself when talking to others. In many ways, tradition is intertwined with other concepts we've discussed in this book—culture, beliefs, superstition, and even food.

However, tradition is not just a word. Oftentimes, traditions are living and breathing things that continue to be reconstructed, adapted, and changed with the people who practice them. Earlier in this book we discussed the ways in which we work with plants and ancestral allies as spirits. In that sense, even each tradition has its own spirit that requires relational community as we move through our journey. In certain cases, adaptations of traditions may vary from region to region, such as the evil eye cure in Italy. Each region may have its own particular curing methods based on what is accessible to them, while the prayers and the cure itself will vary from family to family. Upon reading Antonio Pagliarulo's work, *The Evil Eye*, I was surprised at the variety of folk Catholic and even Italian traditions presented within the book—some I had never seen written about while others I had never heard of before. While certain cultures may have traditions surrounding particular saints, holidays, or even modes of healing, the culture itself and the tradition may be adapted, changed, or reformed as it passes through word of mouth or even down family lines. We talked a lot about diaspora and change in food earlier in this book, and understanding the way in which tradition evolves can also be understood in this way. We may know that our great-grandma or ancestors cooked a dish a particular way on a certain holiday, but that it may be due to what the people had access to.

Understanding tradition is an element of reconnection that is vital before we begin to incorporate holidays, practices, or beliefs into our lives. Behind every tradition that we practice is a belief or reason why it began. Why do we throw salt over our left shoulder? Why do we cook lentils on New Year's Eve? Why should you buy a new broom as you move to a new home? What is the importance of the Epiphany and the house-protection ritual within it? At the center of each tradition are the folk and the beliefs that inform why we do certain things. Tradition represents an extension of culture in a tangible and practical way that requires, similar to all elements of reconnection, respect and understanding as we begin to explore it. Respecting a tradition may involve asking more about the background of a particular holiday, food dish, or festival, but also respecting when someone tells you that you are not ready to celebrate a particular tradition or take part in it yet. Similar to methods of initiation and initiatory practices, certain traditions within certain cultures may require you to be of a certain age to participate. You simply may not be allowed to participate in certain traditions as a reconnector due to where you are in your journey. Similarly, we can interrogate traditions we are looking to adapt into our lives for whether or not they maintain problematic elements that do not reflect our beliefs as reconnectors. Certain traditions like Black Pete of the Sinterklaas parade in the Netherlands or the performance of minstrel shows in the United States shouldn't be protected just because it's something people have been doing for a long time. Rather, we should be able to analyze the ways in which we participate in certain holidays or widely held beliefs within culture. Are they inherently problematic? Someone in your family or community may argue no simply because it's the way it's done, even if the way it's been done causes harm or perpetuates harm to another community.

So how do we identify traditions we are willing to implement in our lives and the manner and extent to which we want to do so? Traditions in many forms can be looked at through a variety of lenses, but here is what I consider when looking at traditions and whether or not I want to implement them into my day-to-day life.

WHAT IS THE BELIEF AND BACKGROUND BEHIND THIS TRADITION?

Does this way of being have a particular history, background, or belief behind it that I have to understand before implementing it? How can I access that information? For example, if lentils are eaten on New Year's Eve to bring in abundance and good luck, are lentils representative of these elements in other areas of life? Are they used in different practices in similar ways? Does this belief or the background reflect an intent to harm or target others?

IS THIS TRADITION A PRACTICE?
Will this be something to implement in everyday life, such as a morning prayer, a recipe, or a spiritual practice? An example of this in my practice is particular methods of cleansing and recipes that I utilize in my day-to-day; for example, cleaning by showering the floors with salt while reciting a specific prayer, and laying salt under my doormats to protect the home are both found in different Italian Americans' research of the folk customs and practices of the diaspora.

IS THIS TRADITION AN EVENT?
Is this tradition surrounding a special day, festival, or time of year? An example of this in my practice is *la notte di San Giovanni* or *la festa di San Giovanni*, where many Italians and Italian Americans make *l'acqua di San Giovanni* (Saint John's Water).

IS THIS TRADITION PRACTICAL?
Is this tradition one that is easy to implement into your yearly calendar or one that requires adaptation? Is this a tradition that reflects an older way of thinking or being or that requires materials you don't easily have access to?

ARE THERE ELEMENTS OF THIS TRADITION THAT ARE PROBLEMATIC, HARMFUL, OR OUTDATED?
An example of this could be a certain belief held that is considered "traditional," but is a harmful ideology, or an outdated

way of being that perpetuates wrongful or discriminatory narratives regarding members in your community or another community.

WHAT WOULD THIS TRADITION LOOK LIKE IN MY CURRENT COUNTRY AND AREA?

With certain traditions, a variety of items are utilized that may not necessarily be available to you where you are right now. Is there a way for you to access these ingredients? Will you need to substitute certain food items, plants, or spices in order to participate in this tradition? What would it look like? For example, I cannot find fava beans (broad beans) in my local area. These beans are frequently used in certain Italian American folk practices to divine or to offer to Saint Joseph. The decision then becomes whether I seek out fava beans from abroad or utilize another bean with a similar association as divinatory tools.

TRADITION AS HOLIDAYS

Particular holidays and even festivals can represent an important aspect of tradition that we may take for granted or overlook. Oftentimes, the threads of tradition remain in assimilated families. Even within families that exist within their culture, someone may be embarrassed of their culture while growing up only to appreciate it as they get older. I know many Italian American individuals who pushed away from the culture and even their family only to revisit it as they grew older with a renewed sense of passion and self. Similarly, I can easily recognize diasporic traditions and beliefs that I grew up with despite not realizing their importance or their ties to Italian American culture. Christmas Eve dinners, a Saint Joseph figurine on the mantle alongside other items important to my family that subsequently disappears whenever a house needs to be sold, ideas surrounding bragging and boasting are all ways that traditions persisted within my family and my life as an Italian American outside of the culture. It's incredibly easy to focus on the things we don't have rather than the things we do, yet it's the pieces that remain that assist us in reconstructing and reconnecting with what has been lost over time. Certain holidays may hold particular sway within certain cultures, such as *Día de los Muertos* in

Latin American and Mexican culture, *Walpurgisnacht* in German and German American folk magic, and *Midsommar* in Scandinavian folk practices. Recognizing holidays as extensions of culture and belief allows us to not only understand and respect them, but begin implementing them into our lives.

Recalling what you remember from your childhood as important days of the year is a starting point for reconnection. From there, you can utilize the research section of this book to explore what holidays may hold significance within your culture. Regional and diasporic practices may place slightly different importance on certain days than the institution of the Church or a country as a whole do. Certain areas of your ancestors' homeland, and even your diasporic culture, may have opposing traditions surrounding a holiday than those found in the homeland—we frequently see this in Italian American culture through the Feast of the Seven Fishes, which is purely a diasporic phenomenon. A difference in holiday doesn't represent a straying from culture or mean that either tradition is lesser. Rather, it represents diasporic peoples finding what works for them in terms of accessibility and practicality. What is imperative in recognizing and implementing holidays is the recognition that a diasporic holiday or dish may not represent the holidays and diasporic traditions of the homeland in the same way that traditions from the homeland may not always represent or reflect diasporic traditions.

Holidays, in many ways, represent a gathering of people, family, or community to celebrate a certain event or create certain things. When we are specific with the terminology around "holiday," Oxford Languages describes it as "a day of festivity or recreation when no work is done." Historically, many holidays have been societally accepted as a day that everyone receives off of work while others may be ignored or pushed to the side. Depending on your current region, certain holidays may be formally accepted as days you receive off of work or school while others may need a push from the public to be considered as such. There may also be difficulty in receiving them off at all even as an individual. This is in many ways dependent on the culture and country you currently live in. In America, many regions may only have Christian holidays off while others may have Christian and Jewish, but need a push for Muslim holidays off. Depending on the majority of individuals within your region and community as well as the most publicly accepted cultures or ways of being, you may receive a completely different rest schedule. Participating in holidays that represent your culture not only challenges the ideas of your local community and dominant culture about holidays and what constitutes them, but asks you to hold space for them in a way that may not be accessible for everyone. Asking to take time off of work for Saint John's Eve is a privilege—I know I will be able to make up the day and my income will not take as much of a hit. Other individuals may struggle to take off a day for certain holidays when they are not already given. Recognize that implementing holidays as rest days and days to celebrate your reconnection takes time and privilege, and because of this, be kind to yourself as you begin to research and implement festivals and events true to your culture.

While the specific definition of "holiday" may not encompass it, I frequently include certain daily traditions as part of this category. In Italian American culture, this may be making Sunday sauce. For Jewish readers, this may be observing Shabbat and its rituals, giving yourself a day of rest—or the like.

Certain days a week or month may hold importance and tradition within your culture or even family. Nights during the week may be dedicated to a family dinner when all members are free. Your family may hold a movie night one day every month.

Traditions that ask you to hold space for yourself and your community can easily be counted as "holidays," even if they don't fit into the traditional definition of the word. My family watches Eurovision every year, and we have since we lived abroad when I was in middle school. Your birthday, your family's birthdays, and your community's birthdays easily represent annual traditions in which you automatically rest and celebrate someone around you. Perhaps on a certain family or community member's birthday, you eat a specific type of cake you love. When you gather together for a monthly movie night, everyone has to bring a snack and contribute.

Holidays are both those that we create and those that we breathe life back into after losing them in assimilation. Perhaps you know that a certain holiday is important in your ancestors' culture, but you've never practiced it nor has your family. Allow yourself space to research it, understand the importance of it, then do so. This may be a saint's festival that your grandmother practiced, a larger holiday that your family was never a part of, or something you know was important to the culture of your ancestors that was lost over time and through assimilation. Despite the type of holiday or the way in which you stumbled upon it, allow yourself space to experiment, explore, and learn more about the ways in which your culture celebrated their community and beliefs.

TAKE THE HOLIDAY OUT OF THE INSTITUTION

In the context of certain holidays, particularly those informed by the Christian Church, such as saints' festivals, it's easy to associate the holiday with the Church and the Church's teachings.

The origin of the word "holiday" is even "holy day," furthering the evidence of how Christianity, as the dominant religion in many regions, has created and influenced more than we first realise. In the realms of folk magic and folk Catholicism, the people and the folk themselves can expand upon and create their own holidays with set rituals and importance. While Christmas in theory is a holiday to celebrate the birth of Jesus, many families who celebrate may not even be Christian or the way they celebrate the holiday is intrinsic to the culture they grew up with. Varying folk rituals exist around Christmastime, especially during the days of the Epiphany, such as the making of Three Kings salt (Norman, 2022), house blessings, and particular food dishes like lentils in Italian American folk magic. Other diasporic cultures and folk practices may also have different practices that aren't found in traditional celebrations of Christmas. Similarly, certain folk rituals and folk practices may surround the various feast days of saints, such as the festival of Saint John the Baptist where many Italians and Italian Americans make the *l'acqua di San Giovanni*, or Saint John's Water.

In the same way that people have their own relationships with the saints that inform their experiences as practitioners, people also have their own traditions surrounding holidays that are separate from the religious institution. Allowing ourselves as reconnectors to see certain holidays not only as representative of the original source material, but as traditions that grow to fit the needs of those around them which may not always reflect the institution or the institution's beliefs. Discomfort around celebrating holidays associated with problematic institutions is understandable and valid in many ways—don't feel pressured to begin celebrating Easter or Christmas just because your ancestors did. Rather, see what associations these holidays have to yourself and others in your community, outside of what the institution says about them. Does Christmas remind you of spending time with your family? Does Easter represent a time when spring began and rebirth was plentiful? Does your community participate in certain cleansing or protective rituals at certain times of the year? Did your ancestors' town have certain days or times of year when they celebrated certain elements of their life? Looking at holidays through the lens of the folk rather than the institution does not mean completely divorcing the origin of the holiday from how you celebrate it; rather, it allows you to build upon it as one of the folk and as a reconnector and to form your own understanding and celebration of the holiday.

TRADITION AS PRACTICE

While holidays are one way of implementing tradition into your journey as a reconnector, recognizing the ways in which tradition operates as ways of being, thoughts, or practice allows us to further incorporate tradition into our day-to-day lives. The usage of particular sayings, superstitions, or prayers represents ways of being that reflect long-standing traditions and beliefs that the folk have had and passed down. In Italian American folk magic, the belief in the evil eye, the prayers used to cure it, and the method of removing it all represent greater ideas around how we should treat the people around us. *Mal'occhio* is the belief around the idea of an individual lacking in something, envying or wanting something that another individual has. In many cases, these ideas are referred to as "juiciness" or "dryness"—the person lacking, or the "dry" person, can see the person who is "juicy," or who has something they do not, and then subsequently takes or steals it from the individual through the evil eye. These beliefs reflect ideas surrounding who is more likely to give the evil eye and who is more at risk of receiving it. When we understand the fundamental ideas behind *mal'occhio* in Italian and Italian American folk magic, we can further understand who is more at risk of receiving it and the apotropaic rituals and charms to protect them. Thomas Hauschild explains this belief set in his book, *Power and Magic in Italy*, writing, "Blood is life, death is dry ... To dry out life means to reverse it ... To be cursed means that your blood is bound, it is encumbered with something dry, something tough ..." He further expands on the source of this belief, writing, "If we remove highbrow concepts such as the atom and logic from ancient Greek philosophical writings, there is one teaching on life that remains. It is based on the contrast between pulsating vivacity and the terrible dryness of death. That is the 'emphatic contrast of life'" (Hauschild, 2010). *Mal'occhio* curing and belief in Italian American culture represents one aspect of the ways in which tradition can be passed through both practice and knowledge, representing elements of the culture that we can begin to study or implement into our practice in everyday ways.

Implementing tradition in practice is a step towards actively participating in and contributing to the culture you are reconnecting with. It represents an adoption of beliefs, a rebirth of ways of being, and old practices that may have been lost being brought back into your life. For certain reconnectors, implementing practices that align with tradition may be trial and error—it may be difficult to source information or you may struggle to find the space in your current country and society to safely implement these practices. It's a privilege to not only have the space to reconnect with tradition and belief, but also to not worry about the possible danger of doing so from those around you. Holding space for this privilege as a white reconnector is imperative and allows us to understand the ways in which we can hold ourselves and others accountable for the space we take up and how to make room for everyone in reconnection spaces. Tradition as a practice will look different for everyone reading this book, but here are some ways in which tradition manifests as practice within my reconnection journey:

1. The belief in and curing of *mal'occhio* affecting how I interact and treat others.

2. The emphasis in Italian American folk belief of community as protection—to be loved and to love others is our first step to being protected individually and communally. We see this belief present in the emphasis on gifting. To receive something from someone you love represents an element of protection that extends beyond wearing an apotropaic amulet or carrying a *breve* bag.

3. The belief of brooms as powerful tools and one of the most sacred spaces being the home. In my practice, this manifests in cleanliness, protective measures, and certain rituals within the home to create a safe and love-filled place.

4. The practice and belief of food as medicine and ancestral reconnection. Food is the love language of my family and my mother, my nana, and my *bisnonna* all utilized cooking and food differently to heal and show love to the people around them. For me, it is making sure the people around me are fed and fed well.

5. The practice of venerating and working with my ancestral plant allies and local land spirits.

6. The practice of venerating and honoring particular saints that were important to my nana as well as those that are important to me, as a reconnector. This is especially present in the praying of my nana's novena and the veneration of Saint Anthony of Padua.

7. The usage of herbal medicine and herbal allies in creating healing and protection. This practical tradition

most definitely stemmed from my *bisnonna* but most definitely expanded with my mother. As most of our family is chronically ill in ways that modern-day Western medicine can't always alleviate, my mother utilized supplements (especially those that were herbal) to assist us during our most sick times. As a reconnector, I am expanding upon this by turning to Western herbalism, Italian folk medicine and ancestral plant allies to assist me with health issues that arise, alongside the usage of medication.

This is by no means a section to say that one is better than the other. Both Western medicine and Western herbalism have their dangers and their benefits, and you are not more of a practitioner by utilizing one or the other. Your body is yours and has specific needs that may require the usage of medication or medicines that aren't found in nature in the same way that it may benefit or require the usage of herbal support during trying times. As an individual with a chronic illness who also is feminine-presenting, I often feel ignored or shut down by doctors of Western medicine. My pain or experiences aren't always believed or validated. The institution of medicine and healthcare within my country oftentimes fails those who need it most and has a track record of ignoring the pain of Black and Brown women especially—you may find power in reclaiming the folk medicine of your ancestors or you may get lucky with a doctor you love and find ways of utilizing Western medicine that feel just and fair in your experience.

Tradition in practice may not always reflect a way of being that your ancestors are working to reconnect with, either—for those of us within the diaspora, it's possible we are the product of many backgrounds and feel pulled to one or two of our ancestors' cultures or that a tradition within our current life and practice may not look like either of those. My family has a practice where we kiss our hands then hit the top of the car whenever we safely pass through a yellow light. I'm not actually sure of the origin of the tradition; however a little bit of research reveals that it is relatively common throughout my current country and is often seen as a protective gesture. While this is not a tradition that stems from my ancestors' homeland or culture, it is part of my culture and practices as it is a tradition that I adopted which was passed down from my mother. As we explore tradition as ritual and practice, some of the practices you notice still living in your family may be those that have no ties to your ancestors' culture, but represent the current belief or culture that your family assimilated into. Some reconnectors may feel that these rituals are a source of discomfort and a reminder of the assimilation our ancestors took part in; however I would challenge you to explore and accept these newer traditions as those that represent your life as a diasporic individual. Certain beliefs and superstitions that I hold most definitely come from growing up as an Italian American, but I also know of several other traditions that my family takes part in that aren't necessarily as linked to Italian American culture as others. Some practices you may not even recognize or be able to trace and that's okay. There is an element within the reconnection journey that we have to accept—that our practices and reconnection will not look like our ancestors' because we are not our ancestors.

LETTING GO OF PROBLEMATIC TRADITIONS

The analyzing of problematic traditions and aspects of holidays, practices, and beliefs that are problematic leads to the path of releasing or reconstructing those traditions in a way that fits our current culture and belief sets as reconnectors. This doesn't mean removing all aspects of a tradition that you just don't like; rather it's about recognizing the aspects of a holiday, practice, or belief that no longer reflect our time or ways of being.

The words "tradition" and "traditional" ways of thinking can also lead into long-standing, problematic ideologies surrounding race and gender. How many times have you heard someone explain away their homophobia as "that's the way God intended"? Utilizing and connecting with tradition in your practice doesn't mean turning a blind eye to the harm certain traditions and ways of thinking have done over time—rather, it calls you in to reconnect and release those traditions for future generations.

Numerous traditions may be rooted in antisemitism, racism, or sexism, including traditions that reflect beliefs around these areas, such as Thanksgiving in the United States. Whereas the story taught to young children in schools is that the Indigenous populations and the British settlers were kind to one another and shared food, the actual treatment of

Indigenous populations on Turtle Island is overlooked—specifically, the attempted genocide of Indigenous peoples, the scrubbing out of their languages, culture, and way of life, and the discrimination that they continue to experience to this day by way of settler ideologies and racism. Indigenous women are two and a half times more likely to be the victim of violent crimes, especially sexual violence (Amnesty International, 2011). A lack of media coverage, barriers to receiving justice, and prevailing stereotypes around Indigenous individuals leads to a continued and prevalent violence against Indigenous women, girls, and two-spirits (Native Hope, 2025).

Similarly, some holidays have problematic roots and over time fundamentally change to a point where the origins of the holiday may no longer be seen or recognized. Many settlers on Turtle Island refuse to recognize or are wholly unaware of the harm that is continually perpetrated against Indigenous communities by settler and colonial ideology, yet every year Thanksgiving is celebrated as a "time to be thankful" and "gather with family." Schools often teach a romanticized history of Thanksgiving, and the commercialization of the holiday has led to a focus on eating turkey and staging Thanksgiving parades, while the real Thanksgiving facts show that there's no evidence that the Wampanoag people (the tribe often referred to as feasting with the settlers) were even invited to the festivities. The first harvest that we often see as Thanksgiving was followed by European settlers seizing Native land, imprisoning, executing, and enslaving Native peoples (Menjivar, 2019). When we recognize Thanksgiving for what it is, we see a celebration not of allyship, but of conquest and continued discrimination. Recognizing the problematic history behind this federal holiday allows us to acknowledge the harm this holiday has done over time as well as pay reparations to Indigenous people. As a reconnector, we are already facing accountability and recognizing the ways in which our ancestors and/or current country perpetrate harm and white supremacy against minorities, and while settler-reconnectors cannot "release" the harm that has been done against Indigenous communities on Turtle Island by colonial settlers, we can begin to reconstruct and repair.

Many problematic holidays are not those we can just ignore or refuse to celebrate in hopes that it will create healing. To ignore is to be ignorant of the harm that exists towards many different minority groups and people of color often through the systems that your family may have assimilated into. While refusing to celebrate a holiday is a first step, focusing your energy towards and centering the individuals who were wronged on that day allows us to truly reconstruct holidays and begin to take accountability for the actions of our country and our ancestors. Instead of celebrating the genocide of Indigenous peoples, celebrate time with your family and the harvest of the year while donating time, resources, and finances to movements for Indigenous sovereignty, protection of Indigenous girls, women, and two-spirits, and learning directly from Indigenous peoples about what they feel is appropriate from settlers on this day. Spend time acknowledging the true origins of the holidays and educating yourself via books, workshops, and online articles written by Indigenous authors.

Thanksgiving is not the only tradition or holiday that stems from problematic roots. Different countries or regions may have their own holidays or practices that originated within something problematic. While over time the problematic origin of this tradition may have faded into the background, harm can still persist as the holiday continues to be celebrated with little to no knowledge of its true meaning or origins.

Certain holidays create a space for ongoing hurt—their problematic origins lead to continued harm and further racist, xenophobic or sexist narratives. As reconnectors, recognition of these problematic roots and a push for reconstruction and knowledge of the origins of particular holidays allows us to take accountability for the ways in which both our ancestors and culture contributed to the harm of others.

PUTTING TRADITION INTO PRACTICE

Creating space for tradition in your day-to-day life—this is through the celebration of holidays or through implementing practices and takes time. Practical reconnection can be as simple or as complex as you feel is accessible for you as an individual.

Here are a few exercises and methods to assist you in continuing your reconnection beyond this book.

Gather community together for a holiday or cultural event. Friends, family, or peers are fantastic to gather together to organize an event. This could be a well-known holiday within your tradition, or a newer event centered around communal togetherness and collective learning. Some examples of community holidays or events in my practice and culture include:

1. The gathering of people together on New Year's Eve and Day to celebrate the new year, cooking lentils and other foods together to bring luck into the new year.
2. Christmas and Epiphany celebrations with my family including house purification rituals conducted in honor of the Three Kings, making Three Kings salt.

Sometimes, traditions and practices are easier celebrated alone than with a group of people, even if other people are celebrating it from far away. Some examples of this in my practice include:

1. Celebrating Saint John's Eve or the summer solstice by making *l'acqua di San Giovanni* and doing divinatory rituals regarding the next year.
2. Celebrating certain saints' festivals outside of the Church, including doing novenas or petitions for them.

Sit with your community in ritual, spaces, and classes. Our reconnection is nothing without those on the journey with us, or those who can help us on our journey. Learning tradition and implementing tradition begins by learning about them! Make space and time for connecting with people who hold space for curious conversations and discussion of different practices within tradition.

MAKING YOUR OWN TRADITIONS

As we reconstruct and reconnect, it's possible that a tradition doesn't necessarily feel right for you or that you feel as though your practice is lacking a certain element of your day-to-day life that you feel would benefit from celebrating. This could be the celebration of a newer-established holiday or month that validates you and your identity, such as Pride Month, Autism Acceptance Month, or even Jewish American Heritage Month, or this could be the revamping of an older tradition. You may find that you can't access certain foods that were traditionally eaten on certain holidays and you learn how to create a recipe that's more accessible, or that you want to take an older ritual associated with a holiday or practice and slightly modify it. In the practice of folk magic, this is something that is done frequently. I don't necessarily walk backwards out of my house with inside-out clothes to then strip while reciting a prayer as recorded by Ernesto de Martino in *Magic: A Theory from the South*, which was utilized to reverse and protect against "bad wind." However, I do flip one article of clothing inside out (usually a sweatshirt or sweater) which can easily be removed outside without fully removing my clothes. I will also utilize the prayer within the context of reversing bad wind without actually reversing clothes, such as reciting the prayer over a reversal candle for three days or by itself while walking backwards outside the home. While I would love to completely replicate the ritual every chance I get, the reality is I don't have the ability to remove all my clothes outside due to neighbors. As well as this, I utilize methods of magic in my practice that my ancestors most likely didn't while still understanding and venerating the cultural context the ritual comes from.

Making your own traditions is as much ancestral veneration as it is personal tradition—you may find that you want to honor particular ancestors on their birthday or day of passing by traveling to their place of rest. You may celebrate familial birthdays or events that your ancestors did not, or you may bring older traditions that were once forgotten back into practice. Traditions don't need to be holidays or large events and could be as simple as visiting ancestral allies on a certain day of the month or traveling to a bakery after payday to get certain offerings. To create your own tradition is to fully embrace yourself as a member of the culture and as one of the folk and to recognize the way in which folk magic functions for you, your ancestors, and your community. It is to look around you with the eyes of your ancestors and the eyes of a reconnector, to create something that will be passed down to future generations, and to recognize the ways in which we are healing through reconnection and reconstruction.

PART 5

RECONSTRUCTION

Reconstruction, in and of itself, is a necessary part of reconnection. You will not do things the exact same way that the generations before you did. Your practice will morph and grow. Reconstruction requires us to recognize core beliefs, rituals, and ways of being that have been passed down to us while also asking us to acknowledge that not everything can be duplicated. It's both important and possible to look at how we can grow new roots while staying connected to old ways of being.

WE ARE NOT OUR ANCESTORS

Remember that your practice will not look exactly like that of your ancestors. During my own journey of reconnection, I faced criticism surrounding my practice—not necessarily because I was doing something inherently wrong, but because my practice does not look like the practice of another family's or practitioner's. Authenticity is difficult to come by in a tradition with no formal lineage or way of practicing, variability between regions, families, and even through descendants over time. Even when it comes to practitioners of my own age, I notice certain things that don't feel "right" or that my mother doesn't remember being intrinsic to my family's practice. In a country that wasn't actually a country until the mid-nineteenth century with hundreds of dialects, different bioregions, and different areas of influence throughout history, all manner of ways of being could be considered authentic. Some recipes of red sauce call for white wine and milk while my family's rendition of red utilizes red wine and chicken broth. The writing and pronunciation of *Dio* (God) and *Gesu* (Jesus) varies between regions. Even the patron saint that will be most petitioned varies depending on the town. While there are certain cultural elements that came into being after unification and longer-standing countries may have stronger ties to a unified, country-based identity, there is no way we can completely replicate the practices of our ancestors who existed in a different country, a different time, and a different sociopolitical climate. Folk magic and folk beliefs are of the folk—they morph, change, dilute, and grow through generations. On the journey of reconnection, you are becoming one of the folk. What do you need as you reconnect? Which elements of your ancestors' culture stayed with you through the generations of diaspora while others were shed?

Our practices cannot look exactly like our ancestors' because we are not our ancestors—at least, not exactly. While we carry them inside us and extend their lineages, we are not in the exact same situations that they were—yet some things continue to stay the same. I know I will turn to age-old birthing rituals when and if I choose to have a child. I know I continue to believe that amulets are more powerful when gifted and that the *mal'occhio* continues to persist as an issue I face in the day-to-day. However, I am not an owner of farmland and even if I was, my livelihood may not depend on it. I have access to jobs and doctors that my ancestors did not and a privilege that they put in place. When we strip away how our lives look different, what is at the core of your cultural reclamation? Is it community? Is it protection? Is it justice for yourself and others? Is it a sense of belonging or a feeling of comfort around people who are similar to you? Shed the worry that you are not good enough or that your practice is not perfect and ask yourself what you need right now. What do your ancestors need from you? What does your community and our world need from you? How does your process of reconnection allow you the space to bring back the old, but also invite in the new?

Reconstruction, according to the dictionary, is the action or process of reconstructing or being reconstructed. It is a thing that has been rebuilt after being damaged or destroyed or an impression, model, or re-enactment of a past event formed from the available evidence. We will not know, as reconnectors, everything. We will know what has been taught to us by our peers, our teachers, and our community—but to place together the fragments into some semblance of a shape is our job. We can know what was important and continues to be important within our culture, but perhaps not within our family. We can see the way the fragments form a broken shape, but we may still have some missing. With the information you gather and the people you connect to, you have the capability to work and make your own shape. It won't be perfect nor will it fit exactly into what the other pieces look like, but it will be your shape and your contribution to the continued and fluctuating growth of culture, magic, and belief that informs how we reconnect and who we reconnect to.

In some ways, reconstruction is a practice in both research and intuition. Does this belief feel like it fits? What plants that you connect with and which saints just feel right and provide you with the best response? Can you cross-reference this with what saints or plants grew in your ancestors' town or perhaps were used in their garden? Is this something new, something that exists solely to connect with you as an individual? Things from our ancestral ways of knowing come to us in all manners—but some may not always fit, and you may need to find substitutions or replacements that feel true to your life as a reconnector and as a practitioner. We can be informed by the culture of our ancestors and learn all we possibly can, but when we find an empty space or a missing piece, sometimes we can do with something new. It may not be ancestral, but it may be needed.

Reconstruction also allows us the grace to connect with our ancestors and ask what they feel is missing. It allows us to research, read, and learn then apply our knowledge in a practical way to move forward in our journeys. It doesn't ask us to create something new that goes against the grain, but rather to find something that fits with it and continue forward. Reconstruction is the reality for many reconnectors in their journeys—there may not be any semblance of a culture within their family or it may look completely different to what they read of the experiences of other practitioners and members within the culture. For me, I was not raised in the Church or on Catholic beliefs. Rather, I was raised with the idea that nature was the magic and that we shouldn't take excessively from her. As I continue to reconnect, entities such as saints and Our Lady have made space in my practice, but I approach them differently from how my ancestors did—I don't necessarily think of myself as a Catholic, rather I implement folk Catholicism and entities that can be found in Catholicism in my practice. I am comfortable with the idea of saints being spirits who can help and often utilize them as such. This doesn't mean I don't respect those who consider themselves Catholics or folk Catholics, or that I'm disrespectful of saints as Catholic entities. I frequently employ folk Catholic or even Catholic methods to connect with them and do so unapologetically as a folk practitioner. Prayers that were never utilized in my family have made themselves at home within my life, but I never let go of the way I was raised around nature which continues to influence my land veneration and work with ancestral plant allies.

Reconstruction also applies when necessity or accessibility require changes to long-standing traditions or practices. In my life and practice, this takes the form of new ways of cooking due to dietary restrictions and autoimmune illness. There are things I know about gluten-free pasta such as the best brands, how to make sure the pasta doesn't stick, and how to thicken a sauce in the absence of gluten-free flour. Similar to my nana, who learned how to bake the best biscotti without gluten for us when I was younger, disability has caused my way of cooking and my cooking tricks to adapt and change over time. In many respects, I am reconstructing certain ways of my ancestors while also reforming my practices to better reflect my current needs and what is accessible to me. While this may not reference the exact definition of the word, reconstruction sometimes requires us to reform and revisit older or long-standing practices for a variety of reasons.

ANCESTRAL BELIEF THROUGH A MODERN LENS

Just as our practices will not look like our ancestors', our beliefs will not look exactly like our ancestors'. Recognizing that some beliefs may be shed, morph, or change over time, just as our practices and culture do, is inherent to recognizing the ways in which the beliefs of our ancestors may do so within our generation. These beliefs may be those about the universe and spirituality or simply ethical questions or political beliefs. Belief and ideas will morph like our practices do—based on necessity, social climate, and the people around us. Looking at how our ancestors did things or their common beliefs requires both an analytic and a modern lens. Is this belief true to my current social sphere? Is it problematic or inherently harmful, such as the idea that virgin women or female-presenting individuals are pure due to not yet having sex which presents not only a patriarchal but a sex-phobic way of thinking. We should not grow up to think exactly like our parents or grandparents, but rather learn from them and adapt as we move forward through a seemingly different life. My ancestors never had to form opinions about climate change or the behavior of late-stage capitalism. My ancestors chose survival and perseverance, and because of them I have the privilege and ability to interrogate ideals that they spent their whole life accepting.

Analyzing ancestral belief and widely accepted beliefs of your ancestors' culture requires us to look at several aspects of it:

- What is this belief? What elements of life did it pertain to? Was it spiritual, cultural, or social?

- Why is this belief important? How did it inform the lives, culture, and practice of our ancestors?

- Where did this belief come from? Is it linked to a way of being or a wider social phenomenon?

- When was this belief held? Is this a way of being that has since been shed by the dominant society? Is it still held by some people? If so, do you agree with it and do you feel it serves you in your current sociopolitical climate?

Very frequently, ancestral belief is informed by the culture and society around it. While certain beliefs and ways of being, such as respecting our elders and prioritizing our community, are helpful, some may no longer fit or be useful within the society we are in. For example, I can understand that my ancestors were part of their family and a village before they were individuals—the good of the family and the good of the community came before the good of the individual. However, as an adult in a late-stage capitalist society, this belief is difficult to fully implement. I can love, cherish, and prioritize my family within my life, but I also recognize that my individuality as an Italian American and as someone who has to work to live is important. There is an aspect of this that also reflects my life as a diasporic person—I am not in the same environment as my ancestors, so I struggle to follow in their footsteps in their entirety. I was raised in a diasporic culture that branched from the original beliefs and ways of being of my ancestors, but is not exactly the same. In more ways than one, this morphs and changes our belief systems. There are numerous beliefs that my ancestors most likely held that I continue to implement in my life, such as the prioritization of community, the importance of food and home, and the way I interact with people as well as spirituality. However, I don't necessarily follow the inherently Catholic or patriarchal beliefs that my ancestors also may have held. I continue to form my own beliefs based on my experiences with the world and the people around me independently from my parents, despite continuing to prioritize their presence and wisdom in my life.

Through an analytic lens, we can identify why certain beliefs existed and why they may not have persisted as our ancestors assimilated or through the generations. When we view ancestral beliefs through a modern lens, we utilize the capability of not only reconstruction but research and cross-referencing to reframe or repurpose certain beliefs. An example of this in my own practice is the way I conduct myself and my protective practices through social media. As someone who exists on the internet, I am perceived more frequently, and to a degree that my ancestors would have never imagined—especially as an individual who openly talks about their reconnection journey online. There are not necessarily any protective measures, charms, or spells that are specifically geared towards social media, nor are there any beliefs surrounding how to conduct oneself on it. While the belief that secrecy and privacy give power to the formulas and cures I utilize continues on within my practice, I am faced with a problem that is unprecedented historically and culturally. Thus, there are aspects of my practice, specifically protection, that would not have been found in my ancestors' lives. There are spirits I willingly work with that I doubt my ancestors would have thought were appropriate, and certain protection rituals and charms that have evolved within the diaspora as well as my personal practice that may be similar to yet not the same as my ancestors'.

> ### Be a better ancestor
>
> *Beliefs can also change as we shed older and problematic notions—while antisemitism, racism, and misogyny may have been "just the way it was" for our ancestors or incredibly prevalent in their country's culture, we can create awareness around how continuing these beliefs is problematic. Taking a further step, we can look at the ways in which certain traditions or practices may have been formed as a result of these problematic beliefs and recognize that through a modern lens, they are inherently harmful to our reconnection journey as well as those around us. For us to reconnect, we are not just reconnecting with culture and our ancestors, but we are choosing to become a better ancestor than those that came before us. Every reconnector reading this most likely had a family member they remember who was harmful or problematic in some way. I often get asked about problematic ancestors or family members when discussing ancestor veneration and reconnection and the biggest question is—what if I don't like my family or have an ancestor I don't want to venerate? Different reconnectors have different responses to this, including a variety of methods for handling troublesome ancestors in your reconnection journey. In my practice, I feel that if*

you don't want to venerate a particular ancestor, you don't have to. Rather, notice what about them has harmed you or the people around you. I will never be one who tells you that you should work with ancestors who have traumatized you, but I will be the one who encourages you to analyze the ancestor in question. Is your push away from them because they personally mistreated you and caused you harm, or is the push away from them a question of morals, where you no longer find their problematic ways of thinking to be reflective of you and your beliefs? If it's the latter, instead of refusing to acknowledge or work with that family member, I would encourage you to make space for not only healing the ancestor but healing the lineage. When we make space for acknowledgment and healing, this doesn't necessarily mean inviting this ancestor or a group of ancestors into our space, seeking counsel with them, or putting them in a place of high veneration. Recognizing the harm that your ancestral lineage may have done through their beliefs requires us to not only acknowledge that harm was done, but listen to minority communities that were harmed by our lineages about how to move forward. This is especially important with settler and white reconnectors as white supremacy and white privilege are so incredibly prevalent that it's very likely you were indoctrinated into certain sets of beliefs or ways of thinking that are harmful. Acknowledging the previous harms our ancestors have done is integral in breaking generational cycles of violence and trauma, allowing us to move forward into creating a better world and becoming, ourselves, a better ancestor for future generations.

PUTTING RECONSTRUCTION INTO PRACTICE

Putting reconstruction and reconnection into practice expands beyond this book and extends its roots into your community and current practice. Here are a few exercises and methods to assist you in continuing your reconnection beyond this book.

Gather people together for an event that your ancestors may not have celebrated. This may be something that is important to you or is a part of your practice, but would not have been celebrated by your most recent ancestors. Examples of this in my practice include:

1. Ancient Roman festivals, such as the Nemoralia or Lemuralia
2. Solstice celebrations and get-togethers to celebrate the turning of the wheel of the year
3. Celebrating ancestors and ancestral veneration on All Hallows' Eve and All Souls' Day, including others in these celebrations

Acknowledge days, people, and celebrations that fit into your current worldview as well as your community's worldview. This could be a queer icon or ancestor, a revolutionary member of your past community, or even implementing ancestors' deaths or birthdays into your practice.

1. Create something new. Take a tally of what you and your community need right now, and create something to assist. Is it communal protection? Is it a spell to ward off debt collectors? What is something that you need right now that your ancestors may not have needed?

2. Breathe life into old rituals and traditions. Similar to the section on page 64 discussing candle divination and seven virgins, recognize that sometimes rituals or traditions are outdated and/or difficult to access. How can we repurpose and reconstruct them in a way that honors tradition, but makes way for something new? Is there a new herbal ally you wish to perform an age-old cure with? Is there an old prayer you feel will fit somewhere else or in a different context?

When we are reconnecting, we learn that the journey we are on is as much about the past as it is the future and what we will pass down to generations below us. This could be children, students, or even other family members who express interest in what we've learned. The biggest question I leave you with is not what do you want to bring back, but what do you want to pass down and bring with you? Do you want generations after you to know how to cure the evil eye? What do you want them to prioritize and take with them as they grow and become an ancestor? How can we implement this into our lives and practices now in a way that is sustainable, ethical, and continues to pave the way for future generations and lineage healing?

CONCLUSION:
THE DIASPORA AND RECONNECTION IN ACTION

Diaspora is reconstruction and "you are not your ancestors" in action. We have the opportunity to make conscious choices in so many ways regarding what we keep and what we change, what traditions we continue to carry with us and what we set down to wash away. Our ancestors may not have necessarily had this privilege; especially those who did not have access. The traditions we know and love often came from necessity. It is a beautiful thing to be able to discern what we keep with us. Populations of people and belief are fluid, and over time will come to adopt new ways of being from their diasporic land. The changes in social behaviors, culture, and in accessibility are some of the main reasons we cannot recreate, to a tee, the traditions of our ancestors. We are completely different people with completely different experiences that may have been influenced by immigration or assimilation over time. Generational drift and the void that is left behind for many when culture begins to disappear is the reason why we reconnect and seek to reconnect. For folk magic and ancestral practices and traditions, diaspora means you're working with an entirely different environment and region from that of your ancestors. Diasporic traditions can branch so far from the original roots that they are completely and utterly informed by the diasporic people even when acknowledging the origins. Diasporic belief and folk magic may be so intertwined that everyone does a little bit of it in the kitchen or to secure a job, despite not being able to distinguish it from day-to-day, mundane activities.

You may not feel pulled at all to the saint from your ancestors' town, but you may find that a saint representing your cultural identity as a diasporic reconnector fits better. You may struggle to find plants that your ancestors easily foraged, instead having to revise and find new allies that sit in similar categories. The ingredients in your cupboard, the cultural holidays you celebrate, and even the cultural mannerisms in your repertoire may be different from your ancestors'. Your practices as a reconnector will change based on what you need, as one of the folk, and what the people around you need within your community. Even then, no one reconnector's life, belief, and practice will look the same as those around them, because like our ancestors we are not a monolith. Each peer and teacher I know of has a different way of approaching a problem and a different tool they use to solve it. Some of these tools may reflect practices of the homeland while others may be those that were used by their mother or grandmother living in the diaspora. Reconnection isn't about being perfect or making sure everything looks exactly like what came before. Culture and cultural identity continue to morph and change as time goes on, as do the folk. Beliefs can be passed down from teacher to student, from peer to peer, or from father to son, but it doesn't mean that that belief will stay exactly the same over time, nor may it even reflect the knowledge passed down in the generation before. Oral traditions and lineages may hold the morals, ethics, and cultural beliefs of the folk over time, but the methodology and ways in which they are applied will change. Your identity and what you value may be unlike those that came before you, challenging you to reconstruct and reconnect in ways that prioritize what you hold dear. You may not celebrate the Assumption of Mary, but rather the Nemoralia; or both. Your cooking may look infinitely different from even your grandmother's, but you know that the love in it is what counts.

"The ways in which we are and are not our ancestors continues to expand every day." The folk, which are the heart of this book, continue to change, grow, and shift while some things refuse to change over time. Reconnection is the chance to reconstruct, return to, and honor ancestral ways of being and ancestral tradition while also recognizing that some things can and should change. That change, of all things, is not bad. We can mourn the old ways and what we lost, but reconnection is the process of mourning in action. It is recognizing how we have fallen away from community and the collective and making strides to return to it. It's listening to our elders, our teachers, our peers, and watching your mother make meatballs. It's slowing down and sitting with the plants that have known you longer than you have been alive, and it's sitting in grief and accountability. It's messy, it's ugly, it's painful, beautiful, and gut-wrenching all at once. It's the hardest thing to decide to do, especially if you know your ancestral ways of being were persecuted.

And yet, you are here. You read this book. You are most certainly on your way to somewhere from here and where you go will tell you more than I possibly can in these pages. I do hope that this book helped you. Perhaps it made you courageous, perhaps it made you cry, or perhaps it solidified a belief that this is where you are meant to go. In any event, I wish you luck on your journey and wherever it takes you. To the ancestors who came before you, the ancestor you are now, and all the ancestors that come after you, *che Dio ti benedica.*

SUGGESTED READING

For readers who feel like they need to delve deeper into the experience of reconnecting as a person of color, as well as those seeking resources on unsettling settler colonialism and more:

Blackwell, Kelsey. *Decolonizing the Body: Healing, Body-Centered Practices for Women of Color.* 2021. New Harbinger Publications, Oakland, CA.

Chakraverty, Michael. "Reconnecting with My Grandad's Heritage as He Began to Forget It". https://catapult.co/stories/michael-chakraverty-reconnecting-with-grandad-heritage-india

Diaz, Juliet. *The Altar Within: A Radical Devotional Guide to Liberate the Divine Self.* 2022. Row House Press, New Egypt, NJ.

Gutiérrez, Natalie Y. *The Pain We Carry: Healing from Complex PTSD for People of Color.* 2022. New Harbinger Publications, Oakland, CA.

Hurston, Zora Neale. *Tell My Horse.* 1938. J.B. Lipincott Company, Philadelphia, PA.

Kimmerer, Robin Wall. *Braiding Sweetgrass.* 2013. Milkweed Editions, Minneapolis, MS.

Monteagut, Lorraine. *Brujas: The Magic and Power of Witches of Color.* 2021. Chicago Review Press, Chicago, IL.

Rudy. "Accomplices Not Allies: Abolishing the Ally Industrial Complex". https://www.indigenousaction.org/accomplices-not-allies-abolishing-the-ally-industrial-complex/

Saldana, María. "I Want to Reconnect with My Indigenous Ancestry. How Do I Start?". https://www.them.us/story/detribalized-indigenous-person-reconnecting-native

Snelgrove, Corey, Dhamoon, Rita Kaur, and Corntassel, Jeff. "Unsettling settler colonialism: The discourse and politics of settlers, and solidarity with Indigenous nations". 2014. *Decolonization: Indigeneity, Education & Society*, Vol. 3(2), pp.1–32.

Teish, Lusiah. *Jambalaya: The Natural Woman's Book of Personal Charms and Practical Rituals.* 2021. HarperOne, New York, NY.

Tuck, Eve and Yang, K Wayne. "Decolonization is not a metaphor". 2012. *Decolonization: Indigeneity, Education & Society*, Vol. 1(1), pp.1–40.
Unsettling Minnesota Collective. "Unsettling Ourselves: Reflections and Resources for Deconstructing Colonial Mentality". https://unsettlingminnesota.wordpress.com/wp-content/uploads/2009/11/um_sourcebook_jan10_revision.pdf

For readers who want to look deeper into antiracist work and lineage healing. Rather than include my own journal prompts, which will inherently concentrate on whiteness, to assist in this area of accountability, I decided to recommend books and resources written by people of color and minority authors on this topic:

Brodkin, Karen. *How Jews Became White Folks and What That Says about Race in America*. 1998. Rutgers University Press, New Brunswick, NJ.
Eddo-Lodge, Reni. *Why I'm No Longer Talking to White People about Race*". 2017. Bloomsbury Publishing, London, UK.
hooks, bell. *Killing Rage: Ending Racism*. 1996. St Martin's Press, New York, NY.
Saad, Layla. *Me and White Supremacy: Combat Racism, Change the World, and Become a Good Ancestor*. 2020. Sourcebooks, Naperville, IL.
Sue, Derald Wing. *Race Talk and the Conspiracy of Silence: Understanding and Facilitating Difficult Dialogues on Race*. 2016. Wiley Publishing, Hoboken, NJ.

BIBLIOGRAPHY

Abramitzky, Ran. "What history tells us about assimilation of immigrants". 2017, Stanford Institute for Economic Policy Research, Stanford, CA. https://siepr.stanford.edu/publications/policy-brief/what-history-tells-us-about-assimilation-immigrants [accessed: 03.04.24]

Adelman, L., Herbes-Sommers, C., Strain, T.H. & Smith, L.M. *Race: The Power of an Illusion*. 2003. [Film]. California Newsreel & ITS, San Francisco, CA. https://www.racepowerofanillusion.org/

Amnesty International. "Maze of Injustice". 2011. https://www.amnestyusa.org/reports/maze-of-injustice/ [accessed: 01.15.25]

Anti-Racism Daily. "Tracing Your Ancestral Roots is Easy When You're White". 2022. https://archives.antiracismdaily.com/2022/02/03/tracing-your-ancestral-roots-is-easy-when-youre-white/ [accessed: 03.04.24]

Baird, Robert P. "The Invention of Whiteness: The Long History of a Dangerous Idea". 2021. *The Guardian*, King's Place, London, UK. https://www.theguardian.com/news/2021/apr/20/the-invention-of-whiteness-long-history-dangerous-idea [accessed: 03.04.24]

Bardswell, F.A. *The Herb Garden*. 1911. Adam and Charles Black, London, UK.

Birnbaum, Lucia Chiavola. *Black Madonnas: Feminism, religion, and politics in Italy*. 2000. iUniverse, Illustrated edition.

Blunt, J.J. *Vestiges of Ancient Manners and Customs Discoverable in Modern Italy and Sicily*. 2006. Kessinger's Rare Reprints, Whitefish, MT.

Crisis, Karyn. *Italian Magic: Secret Lives of Women*. 2020. Karyn Krol-Tiso.

Davis, Angela Y. *Women, Race & Class*. 1981. The Women's Press Ltd, London, UK.

DeBray, L. *The Wild Garden*. 1978. Mayflower Books, New York, NY.

Digital History. "Italian Immigration". 2021. https://www.digitalhistory.uh.edu/voices/italian_immigration.cfm [accessed: 03.04.24]

Fahrun, Mary-Grace. *Italian Folk Magic: Rue's Kitchen Witchery*. 2018. Red Wheel Weiser, Newburyport, MA.

Fazio, Lisa. "Plants and Flower Essences for Ancestral Healing". 2019. The

Root Circle. https://therootcircle.com/blog/2019/2/10/plants-and-flower-essences-for-ancestral-reclamation [accessed: 03.04.24]

Fazio, Lisa. "6 Herbs for Lung Support". 2018. The Root Circle. https://therootcircle.com/blog/2018/11/27/6-herbs-for-lung-support [accessed: 03.04.24]

Hauschild, Thomas. *Power and Magic in Italy*. 2011. Berghahn Books, New York, NY.

House of Good Fortune. "Cimaruta: Magical Rue". https://www.houseofgoodfortune.org/cimaruta [accessed: 03.04.24]

Hufford, David J. "Beings Without Bodies: An Experience-Centered Theory of the Belief in Spirits". *Out of the Ordinary: Folklore and the Supernatural*. 1995. University Press of Colorado, pp. 11–45. DOI: 10.2307/j.ctt46nwn8.6. [accessed: 03.04.24]

Javelosa, June. "Memories can be Inherited, and Scientists May Have Just Figured out How". 2016. Futurism, Brooklyn, NY. https://futurism.com/memories-can-inherited-scientists-may-just-figured [accessed: 03.04.24]

Jheneall, Trecha G. "Rituals of Belonging". 2022. University of New Orleans Theses and Dissertations, New Orleans, LA. https://scholarworks.uno.edu/cgi/viewcontent.cgi?article=4239&context=td [accessed: 03.04.24]

June, Mara. "Blue Vervain: An Ancient, Sacred Panacea". 2020. Resilient Herbalism. https://resilientherbalism.com/blue-vervain-an-ancient-sacred-panacea/ [accessed: 03.04.24]

Krippner, S., Budden, A., Gallante, R. & Bova, M. "The Indigenous Healing Tradition in Calabria, Italy". 2011. *International Journal of Transpersonal Studies*. Vol. 30(1), 48–62. DOI: 10.24972/ijts.2011.30.1-2.48

Kwang-kyu, Lee. "The Concept of Ancestors and Ancestor Worship in Korea". 1984. *Asian Folklore Studies*, Vol. 42, No. 2, Nanzan University. https://www.jstor.org/stable/1178009 [accessed: 03.04.24]

Lalami, Laila. "What Does it Take to 'Assimilate' in America?". 2017. *New York Times*, NY. https://www.nytimes.com/2017/08/01/magazine/what-does-it-take-to-assimilate-in-america.html [accessed 01.15.25]

LaMorte, W.W. "What is Culture?". 2016. Boston University School of Public Health. https://sphweb.bumc.bu.edu/otlt/mph-modules/PH/CulturalAwareness/CulturalAwareness2.html [accessed: 03.04.24]

Long, Stephen. "What Is Culture?". *Theology and Culture: A Guide to the Discussion*. 2008. Lutterworth Press, James Clarke & Co Ltd.

Lui McKinnon, H. "Why Is Chamomile Suddenly Everywhere?". 2023. https://taustralia.com.au/why-is-chamomile-suddenly-everywhere/ [accessed 01.15.25]

Magliocco, S. "Spells, Saints, and Streghe: Witchcraft, Folk Magic, and

Healing in Italy". 2000. *The Pomegranate*, 13 (Summer), 4–22. DOI: 10.1558/pome.v13.i10.14537

Malpezzi, F.M & Clements, W.M. *Italian-American Folklore*. 2002. August House Inc, Little Rock, AR.

Marble Crow. "Chamomile Folklore and Magical Uses". 2020. https://marblecrowblog.com/2020/02/19/chamomile-folklore-and-magical-uses/ [accessed 01.15.25]

Menjivar, J. "Truthsgiving: The True History of Thanksgiving". 2019. https://dosomething.org/article/truthsgiving-the-true-history-of-thanksgiving [accessed 01.15.25]

Migration Data Portal. "Diasporas". www.migrationdataportal.org/themes/diasporas [accessed: 03.04.24]

Miller, Karen Lisa. "The Folklore of Plants: Juniper". 2022. *Bowling Green Daily News*. https://www.bgdailynews.com/community/the-folklore-of-plants-juniper/article_cde49da5-d52b-5678-b268-177f32509917.html [accessed: 05.01.24]

National Criminal Justice Training Center. "Missing and Murdered Native Women and Girls: National Statistics". 2020. https://ncjtc.fvtc.edu/resources/RS01183335/2022-missing-and-murdered-native-women-and-girls-d [accessed: 03.04.24]

Native Hope. "Missing and Murdered Indigenous Women (MMIW)". 2022. https://www.nativehope.org/missing-and-murdered-indigenous-women-mmiw [date accessed 01.15.25]

Norman, Dee. *Burn a Black Candle: An Italian American Grimoire*. 2022. Watkins Publishing, Clackamas, OR.

O'Connor, B.B. & Hufford, D. "Understanding Folk Medicine". *Healing Logics*, pp. 13–35. 2001. Utah State University Press, UT.

Phelan, Jessica. "Italy's fascinating All Souls' Day traditions". 2020. *The Local*. https://www.thelocal.it/20191101/italy-all-souls-day-traditions [accessed: 03.04.24]

Puca, A. "The Tradition of Segnature: Underground Indigenous Practices in Italy". 2019. *Journal of the Irish Society for the Academic Study of Religions*, 7, 104–24.

Quartly, Jess. "The Way of the Gods – Folk Religion in Taiwan". 2016. Taiwan Business Topics. https://topics.amcham.com.tw/2016/07/the-way-of-the-gods/ [accessed: 03.04.24]

Quincee, Dr. "Cult Recovery: 4 Common Red Flags". Traumastery. https://www.traumastery.com/blog/cult-red-flags [accessed: 03.04.24]

Sedgwick, I. "Conifers and Christmas: The Folklore of Pine, Spruce and Fir Trees". 2022. https://www.icysedgwick.com/conifers-folklore/ [accessed 01.15.25]

Shane, Cari. "What Makes a Cult, and How do Cult Leaders Control their Followers?". 2022. *Discover* magazine. https://www.discovermagazine.com/mind/the-psychology-behind-cults [accessed: 03.04.24]

Skerry, Peter. "Do We Really Want Immigrants to Assimilate?". 2000. The Brookings Institution. https://www.brookings.edu/articles/do-we-really-want-immigrants-to-assimilate/ [accessed: 03.04.24]

Snelgrove, C., Dhamoon, R. & Corntassel, J. "Unsettling settler colonialism: The discourse and politics of settlers, and solidarity with Indigenous nations". 2014. *Decolonization: Indigeneity, Education & Society*, Vol. 3(2), pp.1–32.

Steinfels, Peter. "Idyllic Theory of Goddesses Creates Storm". 1990. *New York Times*, New York, NY. https://www.nytimes.com/1990/02/13/science/idyllic-theory-of-goddesses-creates-storm.html [accessed: 03.04.24]

The Lincoln Druid. "Rue - A Misunderstood Herb". https://lincolndruid.wordpress.com/celtic-medieavel-herb-garden/rue/ [accessed: 03.04.24]

Trees For Life.org, "Juniper Mythology and Folklore". https://treesforlife.org.uk/into-the-forest/trees-plants-animals/trees/juniper/juniper-mythology-and-folklore/ [accessed: 03.04.24]

Vaudoise, Mallorie. *Honoring your Ancestors*. 2019. Llewellyn Worldwide, Woodbury, MN.

Vaudoise, Mallorie. "Madonna of the Mountain in Polsi, Calabria". 2017. Italian Folk Magic. https://www.italianfolkmagic.com/blog/2017/5/12/madonna-of-the-mountain-in-polsi-calabria [accessed: 03.04.24]

Vaudoise, Mallorie. "The Magic of Saint John". 2017. Italian Folk Magic. https://www.italianfolkmagic.com/blog/2017/6/24/the-magic-of-saint-john [accessed: 03.04.24]

Vertovec, Steven. "The Political Importance of Diasporas". 2005. Migration Policy Institute. www.migrationpolicy.org/article/political-importance-diasporas [accessed: 03.04.24]

ACKNOWLEDGMENTS

Ancestral Magic couldn't have been possible without a number of people. Firstly, my lovely agent, Rita, and everyone at Orion Spring, especially my editor Jess, who all saw this book in its conception and said yes. To my numerous peer reviewers—Hannah, Zo, Ji Hae, Voga, Olivia, Cristina, Mary Beth, Lisa, Honey, Keshav—you have all made this book what it is. I couldn't have done it without you, especially those who helped me hit my word count in the final days and pushed me to where I needed to be. Hannah, Zo, and Olivia—you allowed me to bounce ideas off of you like a ping-pong ball, and for that I am eternally grateful for what you have contributed to this book.

Thank you to my teachers and peers, both official and unofficial, but especially those who lent me an ear during periods of grief and pain—Lisa, Mary-Beth, Gina, Gigi, and Loretta. I continue to learn from you in new ways every day.

Thank you to Sharon Arnold, who called me in about my language and provided resources to assist me in furthering my journey of learning about unsettling the settler.

A special thank you to my emotional support during this period. My beloved partner, Ethan, who comforted me during the writing process and the tears. Kara Wood, who sat with me and witnessed my grief in an act that pushed me to write harder. The two furriest of friends, who found out very quickly that I loved having company while I wrote. To my parents, who were always ready to set up my old room for a quick writing getaway and inquired lovingly and consistently about updates.

And of course, to Erminia, Antoinette, Maria Carolina, Francesco, Joseph, and all ancestors named and unnamed, known and unknown—thank you for guiding me here. I hold your names with me when I walk, and I continue to be inspired by the ways you assist me and walk with me. I promise I won't forget a biscotti on your altar again.

Thank you to Ruta, Rosa, and Mandragora, Our Lady of the Miraculous Medal and Our Lady, Mother of God, Diana, Hunter and Healer, Glorious in All Her Epithets, Saint Anthony of Padua, Saint Expedite, Spirits of the Crossroads and of the Cemetery, Spirit of the Fox and Rabbit, Fortuna, Mater Matuta, and Mercury, and all of my spiritual team named and unnamed, known and unknown. For the protection you cast, the assistance you give, and the lessons you provide.

CREDITS

Orion Spring would like to thank everyone at Orion who worked on the publication of *Ancestral Magic*.

Agent
Rita Rosenkranz Literary Agency

Editor
Jessica Duffy

Editorial Management
Georgia Goodall
Carina Bryan
Jane Hughes
Charlie Panayiotou
Lucy Bilton

Copyeditor
Elise See Tai

Proofreader
Lorraine Jerram

Audio
Paul Stark
Louise Richardson
Georgina Cutler

Contracts
Dan Herron
Ellie Bowker
Oliver Chacón

Design
Nick Shah
Jessica Hart
Helen Ewing

Finance
Nick Gibson
Jasdip Nandra
Sue Baker
Tom Costello

Inventory
Jo Jacobs
Dan Stevens

Production
Hannah Cox
Katie Horrocks

Marketing
Corinne Jean-Jacques

Sales
Catherine Worsley
Victoria Laws
Esther Waters
Tolu Ayo-Ajala
Group Sales teams
   across Digital, Field,
   International and
   Non-Trade

Operations
Group Sales Operations team

Rights
Rebecca Folland
Tara Hiatt
Ben Fowler
Alice Cottrell
Ruth Blakemore
Marie Henckel

ABOUT THE AUTHOR

Frankie Anne Castanea is an Italian American practicing diasporic folk magic and a folk witch. They've been reconnecting to their ancestral ways, magic, and culture since 2020 and have been practicing modern witchcraft since 2017. They have a passion for creating and sharing Italian American ways of being, animism, ancestors, and spirit relationships. They hope to make reconnection more accessible to a wider audience and create space for community-building by sharing this book.

They've been interviewed by the BBC, Geeks Out, and more, and are the author of *Spells for Change*. They run a small online shop carrying unique, folk-inspired goods and create content on Instagram and YouTube discussing their reconnection and practice. They are located in so-called Colorado, on occupied and stolen Cheyenne and Ute territories. You can find them everywhere under the username **@chaoticwitchaunt**.